*Critical Multiculturalism and Intersectionality
in a Complex World*

Critical Multiculturalism and Intersectionality in a Complex World

SECOND EDITION

Lacey M. Sloan

Mildred C. Joyner

Catherine J. Stakeman

Cathryne L. Schmitz

OXFORD
UNIVERSITY PRESS

OXFORD
UNIVERSITY PRESS

Oxford University Press is a department of the University of Oxford. It furthers
the University's objective of excellence in research, scholarship, and education
by publishing worldwide. Oxford is a registered trade mark of Oxford University
Press in the UK and certain other countries.

Published in the United States of America by Oxford University Press
198 Madison Avenue, New York, NY 10016, United States of America.

© Oxford University Press 2018

First Edition published in 2008
Second Edition published in 2018

Library of Congress Cataloging-in-Publication Data
Names: Sloan, Lacey M., author.
Title: Critical multiculturalism and intersectionality in a complex world /
Lacey M. Sloan [and three others].
Other titles: Critical multicultural social work.
Description: Second edition. | New York, NY : Oxford University Press, [2018] |
Earlier edition published in 2008 as: Critical multicultural social work. |
Includes bibliographical references and index.
Identifiers: LCCN 2018003498 (print) | LCCN 2018005550 (ebook) |
ISBN 9780190904258 (updf) | ISBN 9780190904265 (epub) |
ISBN 9780190904241 (pbk. : alk. paper)
Subjects: LCSH: Social work with minorities. | Social work with gays. |
Social work with people with disabilities.
Classification: LCC HV3176 (ebook) | LCC HV3176 .C75 2018 (print) |
DDC 361.3—dc23
LC record available at https://lccn.loc.gov/2018003498

9 8 7 6 5 4 3 2 1

Printed by WebCom, Inc., Canada

This book is dedicated to those who are inheriting our past and charged with creating our future. We hope this book supports the process of healing and growth so our children, grandchildren, and students will inherit a kinder world.

Love and thanks to our children—Sarah; Jennifer, Nicole, and Jacqlyn; Jackson; Stacey and Joshua—and our grandchildren—David and Jacob; Olivia; Hayley, Natalie, and Clara—who inspire and inform our efforts to disrupt oppression and work with others to create a world with social, economic, and environmental justice and inclusion for all.

At the core of this book is the work of Jose Sisneros, who was a lead author on the 2008 edition. He set the vision and helped shape the revisions. He has been guiding us in spirit throughout the writing. Jose was dedicated to his family and students, taking pride in their growth. He loved that he could continue to speak to the lives of future generations through his writing.

Catherine Stakeman had a lifelong commitment to community change through teaching and advocacy. Across her career she worked tirelessly for social justice and equity. Even as she fell gravely ill, she continued her commitment to fight for equality. She was dedicated to her family, particularly Olivia, her 2-year-old granddaughter.

CONTENTS

PREFACE

So much has changed in the last 9 years. The global context is now recognized in a new way and the complexity of the issues has changed, or at least the recognition of the complexity. We continue to approach diversity content from a critical multicultural perspective, which emphasizes the impact of power dynamics. We worked to keep the central focus as developed with Dr. Jose Sisneros, while adding the global multicultural voice of Dr. Lacey Sloan.

Combined, the authors have more than 150 years of experience as practitioners, researchers, scholars, and educators. With the revisions, the voices of the original authors still provide the base. These voices are expanded with the addition of a new author, broadening the lens and the global reach. We are fueled by the knowledge that the quality of our children's, grandchildren's, and students' lives is dependent upon our ability to heal the wounds and dismantle the systems of oppression. We are also fueled by our passion for advancing antioppression education and practice at all levels. Our commitment goes beyond the writing of this book. Individually and collectively, we are dedicated to addressing growing inequality, the excesses of privilege, and the impact of oppression. Jose Sisneros and Catherine Stakeman reflect the responsibility we feel to be part of creating a more just world. Even as they faced illnesses that claimed their lives, they continued their anti-oppression work through their writing.

The interactive process of teaching is a journey. This journey has changed us. We have taught, written, presented, and discussed critical multiculturalism in multiple contexts. We have taught single-group courses on topics such as practice with Latinos and Latinas, African Americans, and women. We have taught and practiced in the United States, Mexico, Qatar, United Arab Emirates, and Liberia. We bring multiple views on diversity and multiculturalism; each of us, however, comes from a critical perspective, recognizing the impact of power as an agent of oppression.

Our collective voice represents our racial, gender, sexual orientation, class, and religious diversity. Our writing team was African American, Latino, indigenous, multicultural, and white; poverty, working class, and middle class; lesbian, bisexual, and straight; Muslim, Christian, and other; and disabled and currently not disabled. We have all been active in developing curricula and teaching courses on diversity, and we have faced frustration with the difficulty of finding materials to prepare students around the world for critical multicultural practice. As we used this text, we learned with our students that a global lens is needed to expand understanding the complexities of intersectionality from more than just the Western perspective. As a result, with this edition we attempted to include a more global lens that we hope provides a foundation for students around the world.

There are many books on cross-cultural practice and cultural competence. The study of multiculturalism from a critical perspective, antioppression practice, and social justice is still limited. This book engages readers in a process of personal reflection and knowledge building. After a discussion of oppression and the presentation of a basic theoretical framework for examining multiple issues of diversity and unequal access to power are presented in the first chapter, the focus shifts to identity development and critical self-reflection in Chapter 2. In Chapters 3, 4, and 5, specific identity populations are examined, analyzed, deconstructed, and explored within a critical multicultural context. The structural and power dynamics of privilege, marginalization, and oppression are acknowledged and examined. Through the lens of intersectionality, issues of class, economics, nationality, and religion are interwoven.

In Chapter 6 the intersections among race/ethnicity/color; gender, sex, and sexual orientation; and ability/disabilities are examined as they interact with national origin/language, class, and religion/spirituality. Readers are challenged to think critically about these dimensions and how they intersect. The metaphor of a web is used to explore the holistic complexity of intersecting privileges and oppressions along with the structural mechanisms that support the power dynamics that maintain these systems. This model allows us to acknowledge that multiple oppressions are not simply additive in their effect; they are exponential. Chapter 7 introduces readers to practice from a critical perspective, including multifaceted practice in arenas often defined as "wicked problems." Within these arenas, the intersectionality of oppressions often experienced by marginalized populations most affected by these "wicked problems" is considered. Throughout the text, opportunities for self-reflection are interspersed with content on critical multiculturalism, power, and the complexity of oppression.

We bring these issues to life through the use of case examples and a process that we hope engages the reader in questioning their own hidden assumptions, oppressions, and privileges. The concerns, issues, and fears commonly raised by students as they begin to study diversity, privilege, and oppression are discussed. History is viewed through the multiple lenses of a kaleidoscope, and readers are encouraged to recognize the many worldviews that produce these stories. This framework prepares the reader to undertake a critical analysis of oppression and institutional injustices, the impact of privilege, and processes for achieving transformational change.

Because the issues and their contexts are always changing, each journey through this book is different. Readers examine these issues through their own lens, which is grounded in each individual's unique culture, family, community, and history. Each reader's engagement is grounded in their national origin, race, ethnicity, color, caste, tribe, gender, sex, sexual orientation, disability, socioeconomic status, religion, and age or life stage. We wish you a challenging, interesting, and ultimately enjoyable journey. And we invite you to join us in the ongoing work to end oppression and injustice. As Langston Hughes highlighted, when our dreams are beset "with its back against the wall," the dream "must be saved for all" (Hughes, 1994, p. 542). Here we share *Our Dream of Freedom!*

ABOUT THE AUTHORS

Lacey M. Sloan, MSSW, PhD, is an associate professor at University of Vermont. Her early practice and scholarship focused on sexual rights, with a specific focus on sexual violence and oppression against LGBT people, people with disabilities, and other marginalized populations. Her work in the anti–sexual violence movement at the local, state, and national levels included direct services; legislative policy development, analysis, and advocacy; organizational development; and serving as the scientific lead for the Department of Justice–funded Violence Against Women Act Measuring Effectiveness Initiative. She has facilitated initial development and/or accreditation of three bachelor of social work and three master of social work programs in the United States, Qatar, and the United Arab Emirates. Her current scholarship focuses on using indigenous knowledge and decolonizing practice in developing social work education programs in Islamic countries. She is active in designing intercultural exchanges to confront Islamophobia and other forms of oppression using multiple strategies to engage students in Western countries with Arab-Muslim students.

Mildred C. Joyner, MSW, LCSW, BCD, is professor emerita of social work at West Chester University in West Chester, Pennsylvania. Her passion for social justice and empowerment developed while she pursued her MSW at the Howard University School of Social Work in Washington, D.C. Over the last 40 years she served as a diversity consultant and expert speaker on the topic of race relations for higher, secondary, and elementary education, and for business and human service agencies. She has presented over a 100 presentations and trainings at national, state, and local conferences and meetings on the eradication of "isms." As a part of her commitment to change, she serves as the national vice president of the National Association of Social Work in DC; board member of the Chester County Food Bank; and bank director for DNB First in Downingtown, Pennsylvania. She held other social work and community leadership positions that include president and board chairperson of the Council of Social Work, president of the Association of Baccalaureate Social Work Program Directors, and board chairperson of Living Beyond Breast Cancer.

Catherine J. Stakeman, LCSW, MSW, DSW, was an independent higher education specialist and community citizen active in the fight for social justice. She was recognized for her work during the time she served as the executive director of the NASW Maine chapter. She was formerly an assistant professor at the University of Southern Maine School of Social Work, where she developed and taught courses on diversity for 7 years. She has an MSW from Boston College and a DSW from Catholic University in Washington, D.C. She spent many years as a social work practitioner, community builder, and activist, working mostly with children, youths, and families. She has experience in South Africa and Liberia, where she taught in a small remote village. Her scholarship focuses on diversity and multiculturalism at the local and global levels. She has written on diversity, multiculturalism, and global issues and has presented on multicultural issues at conferences and workshops.

Cathryne L. Schmitz, MSW, PhD, is a professor in the Department of Social Work at the University of North Carolina Greensboro (UNCG). Her scholarship focuses on critical multiculturalism, analysis of the privilege/oppression nexus, environmental sustainability, global engagement, leadership, interdisciplinary education, organizational development and community building, and peace building. She is engaged in intercultural global education, knowledge building, and curriculum development. She has numerous publications and is currently focusing in the areas of identity and culture, environmental justice, interdisciplinary knowledge building, and organizational/community transformation. She expanded her focus through cross-disciplinary appointments with the Department of Peace and Conflict Studies and the Program in Women and Gender Studies. She also contributes to and learns from her work in the community and with the UNCG Center for New North Carolinians.

*Critical Multiculturalism and Intersectionality
in a Complex World*

CHAPTER 1

Critical Multiculturalism, Oppression, and Action

An injustice anywhere is a threat to justice everywhere.
—Martin Luther King Jr., "Letter from a Birmingham Jail"

This first chapter challenges the reader to think about the lens they use to view the history, group relationships, and political discourse around the globe. This establishes a framework for the exploration of multiculturalism through a critical lens. Multiple models and theoretical perspectives with a focus on critical multiculturalism and the mechanisms of oppression are introduced as the portal for investigation.

World history is really a patchwork of overlapping stories, perspectives, and worldviews. The history and perspectives presented here go beyond what is traditionally taught. The voices of those who have been silenced and oppressed are brought forward. By expanding the lens and reframing ideas, we find places where histories overlap. Whereas some groups have experienced privilege, other groups have experienced marginalization.

A relearning of history involves a complex knowledge-building process that can trigger multiple responses. The story told in the history books is that of the politically and economically dominant group. Historically the tellers have been healthy and economically privileged heterosexual males who are usually, but not always, identified as white. Recasting and sharing the story through voices of historically marginalized people can feel unsettling and can lead to resistance and disbelief. Taking an expanded view of global history to note the contributions of people of color, diverse ethnic communities, women, people with disabilities, and lesbian, gay, bisexual, and transgender (LGBT) communities can be both freeing and maddening for members of these groups. Responses such as "Where was I before? Why was I negated?" can surface (see Box 1.1).

It is only through a discussion of difference, an expanded view of history, and acknowledging that oppression of some brings privilege for others that we can move toward change. In investigating these issues, we entertain the possibility described by bell hooks (1995) in her discussion of the beloved community. Her vision is one of love; it is one of creating community by embracing difference. We can only create change and a space in which to live together through the discussion of our differences. In coming together, exploring difference, and working against oppression in our daily lives, we create community and welcome the possibility of change.

So explore the expanded multicultural story of the world. Challenge existing perceptions, embrace discomfort, and accept that difference exists. Explore the issues that engender resistance and discomfort. A patchwork of the multiple intertwined stories emerges. This history is so much richer than could have been imagined.

THEORIES AND CONCEPTS OF DIVERSITY, MULTICULTURALISM, AND INEQUALITY

There are many theories and models that can be used to examine the issues and concepts of diversity, multiculturalism, and inequality across the globe. The concept of *critical multiculturalism* provides the framework for analysis in this book. It is a concept that allows us to move beyond the goal of learning about and appreciating diversity to engaging in an exploration of the multiple and complex power relations of difference and the mechanisms of oppression that operate in societies. The examination of multiculturalism and oppression from a critical perspective involves an analysis of the systems and structures that maintain and perpetuate inequality, with the presumption of a commitment to egalitarianism through action.

Structural-Functional Theories

From Plato, Socrates and Aristotle, and Marx and Weber, the debate over the nature, causes, and consequences of inequality continues. Structural-functional theories of social stratification argue that systems of stratification (the ranking of different groups in society in a hierarchy) are natural, universal, functional, and necessary to the social order (Davis & Moore,

Box 1.1
WHAT I LEARNED IN THE CONVERSATION

Professor: Thank you for coming back to talk with this class. What would you tell this group to keep in mind as they explore issues of oppression and diversity?

Yolanda: First, stay with the conversation, even when you are angry and want to reject everything you hear.

Tom: I agree. I remember how angry I was. In my head, I said, "This professor is so prejudiced. She doesn't care what I've been through. She only wants to get her political agenda across." I kept thinking, "Why all the talk about racism?" I did not see it as a problem. After all, I believed that civil rights had changed the way we as a society viewed black Americans, right? Why the talk about heterosexism? The only "ism" that I felt needed to be discussed was ableism. All the others I just did not consider an issue at all.

Yolanda: My deepest frustration in the beginning was that students were unwilling to talk. On the other hand, there was Tom. I must admit that at the beginning of the class, I wanted to strangle him; however, I can now appreciate where he was coming from because of his honesty. My hope is that as students, you will talk about racism and all the other isms, and also how they all intersect.

Tom: When I first heard Yolanda speak about her experience, I thought that she was exaggerating. I felt that she fit the profile of an angry black woman. I felt everything about her and everything she said was just too radical. Looking back, however, I realize that I simply did not understand her; I was really wrong. It is important for students to keep an open mind. Be careful not to judge.

Yolanda: I would like to add to that, Tom. It is also important that students do not take anything said as a personal attack on them. If someone decides to open up about her experience as a black female in a white society, do not take offense; do not shut down. Listen.

Tom: As a white male from an impoverished and isolated rural community, I can tell you that as you begin this course, you will feel as though you have a target on your back. Just hang in there and remember what Yolanda said about not taking things personally.

Yolanda: I was afraid to talk at the beginning of the class because I was concerned that other students simply would not understand. As a woman of color, I was moved to tears by this class. It was painful, but I feel that I have grown because of it. It was extremely helpful that the professor was there facilitating and helping us work through our issues.

> **Tom:** You are not alone, Yolanda. Most of the discussions had me squirming in my seat. I felt very uncomfortable when I learned about white privilege. I felt guilty, although not responsible, just guilty for not recognizing and acknowledging the benefits of my whiteness, my gender, and my heterosexuality—my privilege.
>
> **Yolanda:** It was very lonely those first couple of weeks. I felt that I did not have an ally in the room. The more I spoke up, the more isolated I felt. Then, one by one, other students finally began to speak up. I felt particularly close to the white lesbian students because I felt that they really understood. For the most part, I believe that they were saying, "Hey, wait a minute, this is our struggle too. Let's tear things down. Let's do things differently going forward. How can we change this white male heterosexist patriarchy together?"
>
> **Tom:** Some people are born to fight and others are not. It is important that everyone step out of their comfort zone and choose a battle. Whether you choose racism, sexism, homophobia, whatever, work to change something in your own way. It can be quiet. It can be loud.
>
> **Yolanda:** Tom, I disagree with you there. I do not understand why we cannot work simultaneously on the isms. Why just one battle?
>
> **Tom:** You are right. I realize that they do not occur in a vacuum. What I meant was that we should strive for change. I love to read and watch the news. Eventually, I began to see how everything we discussed in class was happening simultaneously. Although the intersections were not always obvious, they were there and I could see them. Now, I view the world and the news from an entirely different perspective. We are all connected and so are the issues.

1945; Parsons, 1951; Tumin, 1953). By definition, structural arrangements are created by the

> history, culture, ideology, public policies, institutional practices, and personal behaviors and beliefs [that] interact to maintain a hierarchy—based on race, class, gender, sexuality, and/or other group identities—that allows the privileges associated with the dominant group and the disadvantages associated with the oppressed, targeted, or marginalized group to endure and adapt over time. (Aspen Institute, 2004, p. 44)

According to structural-functional stratification theories, resources are scarce and limited and must be won by those with talent. They posit that there are people who are better at important jobs, and so people who are not so qualified obviously need to fill jobs that are not as important, resulting in income inequality. Although the study of social stratification and the consequences of this stratification and inequality raises important questions (DasGupta, 2015), others challenge the basic assumptions of theories that support the necessity of social inequality on the grounds that there is no evidence that social equality is impossible (Doob, 2016; Tumin, 1953).

Critics of structural-functional stratification theories argue that access to resources is controlled by the elite—those in positions of privilege (Tumin, 1953, 1984). Stratification benefits some groups while withholding resources from others. Being in a position of privilege—for example, having wealthy parents or being a member of a privileged ethnic group—gives one access to resources (for example, higher education), thus increasing one's opportunities. The move beyond these theories, which envisions individuals without agency, to ones that assess systems of marginalization and views individuals (and communities) as potential agents of change, broadens one's perspective. Possibilities for change then emerge. Anthias (2001) argues that "it is necessary to develop an analysis which is able to understand unequal *social outcomes*" (p. 387).

Structural role theory examines how hierarchal social systems are maintained. It suggests that once social structures are in place, individuals will follow the role expectations based on their social identities within the social hierarchy (Biddle, 1986). This theory also examines systems of oppression, roles, motivation, and access to resources within the context of an individual's social roles in a particular societal structure. However, as noted by Meyer, "The inattention to collective and cultural aspects of stratification has been a substantial limitation in the field" (1994, p. 731).

Diversity and Multiculturalism

Likewise, the study of diversity, as it is commonly envisioned, can be narrow and limiting. Students often learn about different cultures by reading literature from marginalized groups and participating in bridging activities, which introduce students to other cultures through what Kanpol (1997) calls the four F's—fairs, food, festivals, and folktales—or as Banks (1997) said, "teepees and chitlins." This approach has some value but is not sufficient. Although difference is acknowledged, the difficult issues of power and domination are not addressed.

The term *multiculturalism* can be descriptive and ideological, or it can refer to political policies intended to address diversity. Multiculturalism, as a political concept, originated in Canada in 1971 as an official policy recognizing the importance of immigration and respect for cultural differences (Metz, Ng, Cornelius, Hoobler, & Nkimo, 2014). Several models of multiculturalism exist (see Table 1.1). Conservative, liberal, and pluralist definitions of multiculturalism rationalize behavior, preserve privilege, and conceal the many ways in which power hierarchies protect ideology and

Table 1.1: THE FIVE FORMS OF MULTICULTURALISM

Form of Multiculturalism Multiculturalism	Definition
Conservative	• Focuses on white Western patriarchal culture
	• Believes the Western system is the best and should be imposed on others
	• Believes in economic imperialism, or control of the economies of less powerful nations by more powerful nations
	• Places blame for marginalization on individuals or their community
	• Denies the existence of mechanisms of oppression
	• Ignores issues regarding access to power
Liberal	• Denies the fact that different groups have different levels of access to resources and opportunities
	• Subscribes to a philosophy of "color blindness," which makes racial minorities invisible
	• Ignores class and gender differences
	• Views white male standards/values as the ideal
	• Believes that assimilation is the answer
Pluralist	• Focuses on difference, separate but equal
	• Only recognizes safe and controllable dimensions of difference
	• Shares shortcomings of liberal multiculturalism
	• Values the coexistence of people from different cultures
	• Believes that anyone can make it by working hard
	• Confuses psychological affirmation with political empowerment
	• Does not address socioeconomic status/structural inequality
	• Celebrates difference while ignoring powerlessness, violence, and poverty
Left-essentialist	• Focuses on differences as an essential piece of identity
	• Fails to acknowledge difference within identity groups
	• Believes that authenticity transcends history, social context, and power
	• Has a tendency to romanticize difference
	• Rejects biological basis for differences but downplays the impact of history
	• Believes only oppressed people can possess moral authority to speak about oppression
	• Assumes cultures are equal and there is no bias

Table 1.1:   CONTINUED

Form of Multiculturalism Multiculturalism	Definition
Critical	• Focuses on emancipation • Views identity formation as socially constructed and constantly shifting • Believes that self-reflection promotes changes of perspective • Makes no pretense of neutrality • Works to expose processes that privilege the affluent and undermine the poor • Is dedicated to egalitarianism and elimination of human suffering • Sees class as a central concern as it interacts with race, gender, and other axes of power • Is concerned with the contextualization of inequalities and how power has operated historically • Acknowledges that there are as many differences within cultural groups as there are between them • Acknowledges that power relations shape our consciousness • Acknowledges that ideological inscriptions become imprinted on our subjectivity • Recognizes that culture reproduces power relations and constructs experiences that preserve the privilege of white supremacy, patriarchy, class elitism, and other oppressive forces • Seeks to understand the power of difference when conceptualized within the larger concerns of social justice

Source: Adapted from Kincheloe, J., & Steinberg, S. R. (1997). *Changing multiculturalism.* Philadelphia, PA: Open University Press.

social order (see Kincheloe & Steinberg, 1997, for a thorough discussion). According to left-essentialist multiculturalism, one form of oppression takes precedence over all other kinds; that is, single-identity groups work for themselves in competition with other groups, not in coalitions. For example, the early women's movement failed to address issues of race, class, and sexual orientation. Similarly, the civil rights movement did not address issues of gender, class, and sexual orientation.

Critical Multiculturalism

Critical multiculturalism builds from the work of many theorists, including Freire and the Frankfurt school of critical theory, integrating antiracism theory, race theory, and critical pedagogy. These theories enable us to move beyond the focus on distinct cultures and place an emphasis on understanding oppression in juxtaposition to privilege (Goodman, 2015). A critical multicultural education focuses specifically on raising the consciousness of social groups that are or have been oppressed and the systems that foster that oppression. Critical consciousness—the ability to question one's history and social position for the purpose of confronting inequality—and sensitivity provide a base for the development of critical thinking.

Critical thinking requires analytical exploration, assessment, integration, and synthesis to understand the deeper political, social, and economic ramifications of the information being considered. The learner engages in a process that weaves together self-reflection, knowledge building, and an understanding of the role power plays in framing and maintaining relationships (Giroux, 1997). Neither personal experience nor politics can be ignored. Freire (1991) and Giroux (1993) highlight the importance of drawing on self-knowledge in building cultural literacy and the ability to think critically. Critical analysis embraces the complexity of conceptualizing difference and the layers of systemic inequality. Critical thinking thus provides the necessary springboard for action, emancipation, and social change.

Critical multicultural engagement requires the ability to conceptualize more than one difference at a time because there are as many differences within identity groups as there are between them (Burr, 2015). It is not just about critical analysis but also about taking action to ensure social and economic justice are attainable for everyone. In the movement toward equality, critical multiculturalists work to expose the subtle and often hidden processes that sustain and perpetuate the privilege of certain groups and the processes that undermine the efforts of groups marginalized by race, gender and sex, sexual orientation, ethnic identity, nationality, class, and ability status.

The critical multicultural perspective builds from a variety of social theories that challenge the idea that knowledge is objective and stresses the historical context in which all knowledge is created (critical theory). The notion that social structures are natural and reality is objective and can be measured is challenged, recognizing that oppression is learned, and privilege is conferred and maintained by social structures (antioppression theory). Culture and identity cannot be simplified, nor separated from other dimensions of the multicultural spectrum. Our construction of reality is determined by scripts (i.e., messages) learned from places such as family, school, and the media; it can therefore be rescripted as we open up a space to dialogue with others and understand that "reality" is socially constructed. Each day, we re-create our reality socially, constructing our history and our future as we construct our experience each moment. Our beliefs and fears are also socially constructed (Burr, 2015).

MECHANISMS OF OPPRESSION

Oppression is pervasive, restricting, and hierarchical, affecting society at both the individual and systemic levels. Oppression may be defined as

> a system that maintains advantage and disadvantage based on social group memberships and operates intentionally and unintentionally, on the individual, institutional and cultural levels. (Hardiman, Jackson, & Griffin, 2007, p. 58)

In systems of oppression, differences are used to identify those who will benefit from oppression and those who will be targeted by it (Williams, 2012). Oppression silences the voices of marginalized people and their allies. People often suffer disadvantage and injustice "not because a tyrannical power coerces them, but because of the everyday practices of a well-intentioned liberal society" (Young, 2011, p. 41). Under systems of oppression, certain identity groups are marginalized and denied full rights and opportunities to fully participate in society. "There is no hierarchy of oppressions" (Lorde, 1983, p. 3).

There are generally considered to be core beliefs in oppression: (a) some groups are superior to others; (b) the "superior" group has institutional power (political, economic, cultural); (c) institutional and individual violence and the threat of violence toward people who are identified as members of the "inferior" group are sanctioned; and (d) the "inferior" group internalizes the negative messages about themselves. Both conscious assumptions and discrimination (explicit bias) as well as unconscious attitudes and behaviors (implicit bias) contribute to the system of oppression (hooks, 1997).

It is evident that the whole system seems to conspire to keep the oppression going. At every level, there are those who give themselves the right to be better than someone else (Just Conflict, n.d.).

> One of the most characteristic and ubiquitous features of the world as experienced by oppressed people is the double bind—situations in which options are reduced to a very few and all of them expose one to penalty, censure or deprivation. For example, it is often a requirement upon oppressed people that we

smile and be cheerful. If we comply, we signal our docility and our acquiescence in our situation. . . . We acquiesce in being made invisible, in our occupying no space. We participate in our own erasure. On the other hand, anything but the sunniest countenance exposes us to being perceived as mean, bitter, angry or dangerous. This means, at the least, that we may be found "difficult" or unpleasant to work with, which is enough to cost one one's livelihood; at worst, being seen as mean, bitter, angry or dangerous has been known to result in rape, arrest, beating, and murder. One can only choose to risk one's preferred form and rate of annihilation. (Frye, 1983, p. 2)

Five Faces of Oppression

Young's (1990, 2011) conceptualization of the five faces of oppression—exploitation, marginalization, powerlessness, cultural imperialism, and violence—offers a tool for understanding the types of oppression that groups experience (see Table 1.2). Exploitation refers to those "social processes whereby the dominant group accumulates and maintains status, power, and assets from the energy and labor expended by subordinate groups" (Mullaly, 2002, p. 91). Marginalization is the expulsion of whole groups of people from mainstream society that occurs when dominant groups are defined as the norm; this denies those not in dominant or privileged groups the opportunity to participate in society in useful and meaningful ways. This powerlessness results in the "placement of limitations on the development of one's capacities, a lack of decision-making power, and exposure to disrespectful treatment based on group membership and status" (Mullaly, 2002, p. 91). Cultural imperialism is when the "dominant group generalizes its experiences and culture, and uses them as the norm" outside their own culture (Mullaly, 2002, p. 91). Finally, violence and the threat of violence serve to keep marginalized groups stigmatized and intimidated.

The struggle against oppression is often met with violence by the oppressors, which results in the dehumanization of the oppressed (Freire, 1985). The oppressors also suffer from the "psychic and ethical violence" of oppression (Bell, 1997, p. 7). The process of oppression hurts both the oppressed and the oppressor (Bell, 1997; Freire, 1985).

Because oppression operates on three levels—individual, institutional, and cultural/societal—change must occur on multiple levels simultaneously (Hardiman & Jackson, 1997). The process of change begins with the development of critical consciousness and sensitivity. That consciousness and sensitivity must then be used to move to action (Freire, 1985; hooks,

Table 1.2: THE FIVE FACES OF OPPRESSION

Face	Definition	Example
Exploitation	The products of the labor of one social group are transferred to benefit another group. Social rules defining work, who performs the work, the compensation for work, and the social process by which the results are appropriated operate to enact relations of power and inequality.	Migrant laborers, primarily people of color, harvest produce for low wages with few or no benefits. This keeps the cost of produce low.
Marginalization	Whole groups of people, the marginalized, are denied the opportunity to participate in social life and thus can be subjected to severe material deprivation and even extermination.	A building does not have the ramps and elevators that a person in a wheelchair needs to enter and get around.
Powerlessness	Marginalized groups lack authority, status, and sense of self.	Single mothers receiving public assistance are treated with disrespect.
Cultural imperialism	The culture and experience of the dominant group is established as the norm. All others are judged by this standard of normalcy.	Relationships in non-white communities are judged by white middle-class norms and values.
Violence	Groups are subjected to physical violence, harassment, ridicule, intimidation, and stigmatization. Direct victimization results in intimidation and the constant fear that violence may occur solely on the basis of one's membership in or identification with the group.	Gay youths are often verbally harassed and physically threatened in their schools.

Source: Adapted from Young, I. M. (1990, 2011). *Justice and the politics of difference.* Princeton, NJ: Princeton University Press.

1994). The process of bringing critical consciousness and sensitivity to meaningful practice is what Freire called "praxis." Integral to the concept of praxis is the development of skills for critical analysis, which views "reality as process, as transformation, rather than as a static entity—thinking which does not separate itself from action" (Freire, 1985, p. 81).

Systems of oppression are maintained through practices that do not question "the assumptions and underlying institutional rules and the collective consequences of following those rules" (Young, 2011, p. 41). The challenge is for those who have been oppressed to resist persistent oppressive forces, regain their humanity, and create change without perpetuating similar power hierarchies and using tactics of oppression like those of the current oppressors. Of course, those who are in positions of power must join with the oppressed to restore the humanity of both the oppressed and the oppressor (Freire, 1985). The dismantling of oppression is a mission for everyone.

Imperialism, Colonization, and Racism: Multiple Threads of the Same Story

Global migration out of Africa is believed to have begun almost 60,000 years ago. By 25,000 years ago, humans inhabited the Americas, Australia, Asia and the Pacific Islands, and Europe. Human movement around the globe, of course, did not stop there. Although there have been waves of colonization since antiquity, modern colonization, as an expression of European imperialism, began in the 15th century. Europeans began to search for ocean trade routes to China that led them west to the Americas, south to Africa and India, and east to the Pacific.

By the time the English arrived in the Americas, the Spanish had already explored (and ravaged) much of the southern Americas. Colonization in the Americas was accomplished through conquest, with indigenous populations decimated by disease, rape, enslavement, and mass killings. European imperialism also included enslavement of millions of West Africans who were transported across the Atlantic to provide labor to meet European demand for sugar, coffee, tobacco, and cotton.

Colonization is based on racism and the idea that white people are superior to non-white people. When western Europeans arrived in the Americas, India, Africa, and Asia, indigenous cultures already had deep and settled roots. Despite that, the newcomers, who came as conquerors, indentured servants, slaves, adventurers, settlers, and merchants disrespected and ignored the integrity of the indigenous communities. Seeing the indigenous populations as uncivilized, colonizers from western Europe chose to dominate rather than collaborate with local populations (Takaki, 2008; Zinn, 2015).

Following conquests of indigenous peoples, the language and religion of the colonizers were usually established as the primary language and religion, respectively. In the Americas and Australia, colonization (occupation) resulted in the genocide of indigenous populations and the theft of indigenous lands. In Southeast Asia and southern Africa, colonization resulted in systems of racial segregation (apartheid) that segregated facilities, housing, and education for whites and non-whites. In India, colonization subjugated the indigenous population, resulting in systematic impoverishment.

Globally, privilege and access to rights continue to be tied primarily to whiteness; this concept has been socially constructed and defined by law in many countries (Lopez, 2006). For example, in both the United States and southern Africa, specific rights and/or privileges were legally granted to those who were deemed "white" and were withheld from others. Whiteness was not simply the product of European heritage or a fair complexion, and wealthy people of color with enough money could pay to enjoy some of the privileges enjoyed by whites. For example, throughout most of the 1800s, Irish immigrants in the United States were considered to be non-white and were relegated to housing and jobs alongside free blacks. The Irish finally established themselves as white by separating themselves from blacks by participating in the oppression of their black neighbors (Ignatiev, 2009).

Discourse of Division

Although there has been critique of diversity and multiculturalism for decades, the backlash has increased since the new millennium. Multiculturalism has been portrayed as stifling debate, fostering separatism, denying problems that exist in minority communities, thwarting the development of common values, and even providing "a haven for terrorists" (Vertovec & Wessendorf, 2010, p. 11). In the United States, since the so-called Contract with America in 1994, conservative pundits have aligned multiculturalism with anti-American ideals; and dialogue on political correctness has served to rally a backlash against discussion of the strengths of diversity.

> Public discourse across the United States and Europe has seen the emergence of the new realism . . . characterized by what its proponents see as the courage to confront taboos, break silence, intervene "with guts" and speak the truth surrounding societal ills hidden by a (leftist) consensus of political correctness. (Vertovec & Wessendorf, 2010, p. 13)

In Europe, this backlash has all but eliminated the word *multiculturalism* from public policy, albeit replaced by the words *diversity* and *intercultural*. Fortunately, the backlash does not seem to have caused public opinion about the importance of multiculturalism and/or diversity to wane (Vertovec & Wessendorf, 2010).

There are many ways that countries become culturally diverse: geography, immigration, occupation, and colonization. In some countries, diversity is portrayed as unsettling and disruptive to the status quo. This results in negative responses to newcomers, with fears about security, employment, use of resources, and changes to the country's core values. Recently we have seen thousands of migrants die in the Mediterranean as they try to reach the safety of Europe, re-engaging the world in the debate about immigration. Citizens of countries receiving immigrants and refugees sometimes complain that the newcomers receive better benefits than citizens who are experiencing poverty, seeing the newcomer as taking precious resources from them. This can result in conflicts between newcomers and others who also experience discrimination and oppression in the country.

It is often difficult to recognize the inherent privilege of being white or light-skinned, male, heterosexual, or a citizen of the country where one lives. Questioning and disrupting institutional norms, identity, and assumptions often leave us confused and anxious. The recognition of this led Freire (1985) to examine the role of education in the development of critical consciousness and sensitivity. Bringing assumptions that lead to the production and maintenance of structures of domination that enforce oppression out into the open offers the possibility for creating alternative structures through the reorganization of social and political life.

Fortunately, social order is not a static given, but a fluid condition to be worked upon and changed (Freire, 1985). Social movements grow from the cultivation of critical consciousness; critical multicultural education can become a tool for change. The foundation of critical consciousness, which characterized early social movements, supports the unveiling of assumptions underlying institutional rules, structured identity, and the collective consequences of these rules. These assumptions are embedded in unquestioned norms, habits, and symbols. "Systemic restraints on groups are not necessarily the result of a tyrant but rather structural. . . . [They are] the result of a few people's choices or policies" (Young, 2011, p. 41). Behaviors and attitudes that serve to preserve the oppression–privilege interchange are entrenched and hidden in the ordinariness of everyday life.

> Societies became what they are through the actions, relations, and consciousness of their members, and they are reproduced through people's socialization and conformity to previously institutionalized patterns of actions, relations, and consciousness. (Gil, 1998, p. 57)

As we develop a critical consciousness, it becomes possible to recognize that as privilege is maintained, the assumption of normality of the privileged group is internalized. For instance, heterosexuality carries the unconscious assumption that it is heterosexual sexuality that is "normal." This assumption can be challenged as LGBT individuals and allies speak out and confront prevailing assumptions of normality. Similarly, as we begin to understand that the dominant group constructs history, thereby defining normality, we can start to dispute such privilege (see Stone & Kusnick 2013; Zinn, 2015).

POLITICAL, LEGAL, AND ECONOMIC INEQUALITY: IT ALL COMES TOGETHER

The political economy of capitalism practiced in most of the world requires systems of oppression and inequality; these systems facilitate the exploitation of the many, which allows wealth to be concentrated in the hands of the few. The accumulation of wealth is often exacted through land acquisition and the systematic subjugation of people of color and other marginalized groups. Marginalized people, those who have been historically oppressed, are structurally disempowered through being denied the resources they need to survive. The political capital of the wealthy is often used to influence the political process and the making of laws (Xin, 2012). Legislation, law, and public policies are used around the globe to limit the rights of the "other"—people of color, women, people who are gay or lesbian, people with disabilities, and so on—and ensure wealth remains with the few.

The impact of inequality has resulted in an expanding income and wealth gap between white men, women, and people of color. As of 2016, Oxfam indicated that 85 people owned as much wealth as that owned by the 3.6 billion people in the bottom 50% of the global wealth continuum; by 2017, that wealth was held by only eight men (six are American) (Oxfam, 2017). In the United States, white men still have higher incomes than men of color and all women (Patten, 2016). Economic inequality is linked to poor health outcomes—from life expectancy to infant mortality and obesity; economic inequality appears to lead to worse health outcomes for both rich and poor. Economic inequality also reduces access to many other resources for those who are in the bottom. For example, in Vietnam, only 7% of ethnic minority households have access to improved sanitation, while among the majority Kinh and Chinese groups, 43% have access to sanitation (Melamed, 2012).

The following examples illustrate how colonialism; institutionalization of hierarchies based on social identities; law, legislation, and public policy; and/or violence or threats of violence have been used to marginalize and oppress certain populations, resulting in economic and social inequality.

United States (US)[1]

Beginning with the Declaration of Independence in which Native Americans were referred to as "savages" for whom the crown was failing to provide adequate protection, oppression based on race, gender, sexual orientation, and national origin has been part of the fabric of life in this country. The framers of the US Constitution were white male landholders who limited access to rights to white male landholders; fortunately, the Constitution itself was framed liberally. This liberal framing has allowed new legislation—including amendments to the US Constitution—to expand rights and privileges of women and people of color.

For example, despite the fact that men of African descent received the right to vote when the Fifteenth Amendment to the Constitution was ratified in 1870, it was only after the Voting Rights Act of 1965, and subsequent related Supreme Court rulings between 1965 and 1969, that many African Americans were able to exercise their Fifteenth Amendment rights. Similarly, although the Fifteenth Amendment banned discrimination to vote based on race, Native Americans were not granted citizenship in 1924. Even though Native Americans were granted citizenship, it was also the Voting Rights Act of 1965 that removed many barriers inhibiting the right to vote. Nonetheless, there remain many barriers to voting for both blacks and Native Americans, including the recent implementation of voter suppression laws in many states.

> These laws lead to significant burdens for eligible voters trying to exercise their most fundamental constitutional right. Since 2008, states across the country have passed measures to make it harder for Americans—particularly black people, the elderly, students, and people with disabilities—to exercise their fundamental right to cast a ballot. These measures include cuts to early voting, voter ID laws, and purges of voter rolls. (American Civil Liberties Union, n.d.)

The US judicial system has also been used to curtail the rights and freedom of various groups throughout the country's history. For example, *Plessy v. Ferguson* established de jure segregation of black and white students with the "separate but equal" doctrine in 1896. This ruling was not overturned until *Brown v. the Board of Education* in 1954. Even then,

---

1. Going forward in this book, United States of America will be shortened to United States (US) by which it is commonly known.

one county in Virginia closed its public school system rather than allow racial integration. And it was not until 1967 that *Loving v. Virginia* established that states could not deny an individual the right to marry a person of a different race. It was not until 2000, however, that the last state law (in Alabama) banning interracial marriage was overturned. The country is still suffering the negative consequences of legalized segregation.

The racism experienced by Chinese and Japanese immigrants and Chinese and Japanese Americans was accomplished through federal legislation and executive orders. The Chinese Exclusion Act of 1882, the first law establishing an immigration quota based on race, excluded Chinese individuals from immigrating to the United States for 10 years. The act was not repealed until 1943 when the United States agreed to allow 105 people of Chinese descent to immigrate each year, regardless of their country of origin. Executive Order 9066 authorized the internment camps for citizens of Japanese heritage during World War II (Chinese Exclusion Act, 1882).

Fortunately, there are ways to challenge institutional oppression. For example, 6 years after Arizona passed a harsh anti-immigrant law (SB 1070) requiring law enforcement to inquire about immigration status if they thought a person was in the state illegally, the Supreme Court struck down three of the five provisions. Alabama and Georgia, states that also passed similar laws, rescinded their laws after a 40% shortage in agriculture workers devastated farmers trying to harvest their crops. More recently, California passed legislation prohibiting state-funded travel to states that have laws discriminating on the basis of sexual orientation or gender identity; this includes Texas, Alabama, Kentucky, South Dakota, Tennessee, North Carolina, Mississippi, and Kansas. The University of California already stopped basketball matches between themselves and the University of Kansas.

Brazil

Like other parts of the Americas, when the Portuguese arrived in what is now known as Brazil, the land was occupied by millions of indigenous people. Also like other parts of the Americas, indigenous people were soon killed, either by disease or by the Portuguese. Brazil's history of colonialism and slavery has created a country whose national identity is racially mixed (Nolen, 2015). When slavery was abolished in 1888, people who were black outnumbered people who were white; there was also a significant population of people who were mixed. Unlike the United States, Brazil adopted no segregation laws, with the idea that Brazilians of all colors were equal (Gradin, 2010).

Portuguese colonization left a legacy of social discrimination characterized by extreme social inequalities based on race for which the federal government, in an effort to reduce the inequality, has adopted affirmative action plans in education or employment (Gradin, 2010). Through progressive social policies and an oil boom, Brazil has seen "more than 30 million people, nearly a sixth of the population . . . moved out of poverty into the lower middle class" (Nolen, 2015). Unfortunately, massive disparities remain between wealthy white Brazilians and former slaves— who had no education, land, or assets (Nolen, 2015).

In 2003, the Ministry for the Promotion of Racial Equality was created to oversee the implementation of affirmative action and antidiscrimination laws. This included laws banning hate speech, and nondiscrimination laws in hiring, housing, and education (Nolen, 2015). By 1996,

> there was a national human-rights action plan, and it included a directive on the need to compensate black people for slavery, although no plan for how to do it. (Nolen, 2015)

In 2004, the University of Bahia decided that 36% of seats would be reserved for black and mixed-race students (Nolen, 2015). The federal government followed suit with affirmative action policies that would reserve 20% of jobs in state governments for people who are black or mixed race (Nolen, 2015). The National Council of Justice reserved 20% of judicial appointments for black applicants.

But after 13 years of these policies, Brazilians who are black and of mixed race earn 42% less than those who are whites (Nolen, 2015). Persons of African heritage experience higher rates of poverty: 37% compared to 17% for those who are white. Brazilians who are black and of mixed race are less likely than those who are white to graduate from high school; people who are black are more likely to die younger and at higher rates. As the income gap between people who are white and black and people who are of mixed race has decreased, the incidence of violence against people who are black has risen (Nolen, 2105).

United Arab Emirates

The United Arab Emirates (UAE) is an interesting country in which to examine the impact of colonization and institutionalization of hierarchies based on social identities; law, legislation, and public policy; and/or violence or threats of violence to marginalize and oppress certain populations. The UAE, a rapidly developing country in the Arab Gulf, incorporated equality for all—including women—in their original 1972 constitution. Previously a British protectorate, the parliamentary monarchy wanted to ensure that they would have the best of everything, including the best social welfare system. The current welfare system provides citizens extensive benefits, including national health care, social security, subsidized utilities, free land upon which to build a home, protections for elders and children, relief from private bank home mortgages, and even subsidies for the often extravagant wedding ceremonies.

Federal and/or state legislation, decrees, ministerial resolutions, and/or adoption of United Nations conventions are some of the ways the UAE government defines public policy in the country; public policy impacts the status of women, workers, and other historically oppressed populations. The UAE adopted many of the United Nations conventions that protect and guarantee rights for women, children, workers, and other historically marginalized populations. At the same time, they have held back the adoption and implementation of certain articles due to perceived conflict with the tenets of Islam. For example, the UAE acceded to the Convention on the Elimination of All Forms of Discrimination Against Women (CEDAW), but it reserved adopting or implementing several articles, including Article 9 (acquisition of nationality). When CEDAW was originally acceded by the UAE in 2004, Emirati women could not pass on citizenship to their children; citizenship could only be passed on through Emirati men. However, in 2012, by presidential decree, the UAE changed their citizenship laws to allow Emirati women to pass citizenship to their children.

The majority of UAE residents are foreign workers; only about 15% of the country's population is Emirati citizens. To protect the rights of workers, the UAE adopted nine major International Labor Organization conventions, followed by passage of federal legislation to protect workers' rights, including in the areas of recruitment, pay, housing, and health (Embassy of the United Arab Emirates, 2017). Yet the UAE (and other Arab Gulf countries) are often identified as failing to protect workers from exploitation—especially unskilled laborers and housekeepers. Bilateral agreements with sending nations are one means of protecting workers from exploitation. For example, India will not allow workers to be recruited to the UAE without proper employment contracts that meet India's minimum wage and standards requirements. Although the UAE does not have a minimum wage, their new eMigrate system identifies 400 categories of skilled workers, with minimum monthly basic salaries (this does not include accommodations, transportation, and other allowances) ranging from 800 to 2,000 dirhams per month (equivalent to approximately 217 to 545 US dollars) (Khaleej Times, 2016).

The UAE Labor Law, or Federal Law No. (8) of 1980, does not protect workers from discrimination based on race, gender, or disability (other than equal pay requirements for women). There is positive discrimination toward Emiratis, who have priority in recruitment and receive benefits not usually afforded to guest workers. For example, Emiratis are protected from termination except under specific circumstances; termination of an Emirati may require the approval of the Ministry of Human Resources and Emiratisation (Al Tamimi and Company, 2017). According to some sources,

> the concentration of wealth is so drastic that less than 0.2 percent of the population controls 90 percent of the wealth. Income and other economic inequalities are a distinct feature of the UAE socio-economic system, and they often overlap with ethnic origins or other divisions in the country's population. The difference in income, even in the same job, between employees with the same qualifications can be large. And the lowest wages are typically reserved for the most difficult and demanding unskilled labour, usually with much lower benefits than those enjoyed in skilled labour or white-collar jobs. (Populations, 2017)

As a result, many jobs are advertised with restrictions or preferences based on nationality and gender. This results in people from certain countries being pigeonholed into certain jobs. For example, Filipino women are expected to work as housekeepers, whereas men from Sri Lanka, Bangladesh, India, and Pakistan are most likely to work in the lower rungs of the work sector.

A CALL TO ACTION

Hope for the future exists in the transformative nature of people (Freire, 1997). Social movements can facilitate social change as the shift in critical consciousness occurs (Gil, 1998). In the 1960s, the United States witnessed the rise of new social movements, resulting in the Civil Rights Act designed to protect African Americans from discrimination in education and employment. More recent global social movements have resulted in increased rights for people with disabilities; gay, lesbian, and/or transgender people; and for immigrants. The Arab Spring—brought forth by youth through the use of social media—saw revolutions in Tunisia, Libya, Syria, and Egypt.

Collective identity and action are necessary for the transformation needed to end oppression and inequality. For transformation to occur, historically oppressed people must be involved in a decolonization process designed to grant them basic rights that should be afforded to all (see hooks, 1994, for related discussion). This transformation is an interactive process that requires the engagement of those with privilege in the growth and change process (Curry-Stevens, 2005). As a significant force in the change process, those who are historically oppressed have the ability to envision, create, and take action to attain justice (Freire, 1997). They must, however, work to develop the knowledge and heart to liberate themselves without becoming the oppressors. This development of consciousness provides a foundation for envisioning transformative action.

However, it is possible for the process of social change not to move beyond the formulation of ideas; in order for social change to occur, "shifts in consciousness [must] cause individuals and groups to evolve new patterns of actions and social relations" (Gil, 1998, p. 57). This evolution depends "on self-transformation by individuals and social groups as well as on institutional transformations carried out collectively by individuals, groups, and networks among them" (Gil, 1998, p. 57).

Unfortunately, people are often afraid of change, which occurs in spurts that are punctuated by reactionary backlashes. The widespread view that "things are the way they are because they cannot be otherwise" serves the purpose of maintaining the position of the economically and politically powerful (Freire, 1997, p. 36). As a result, a culture of silence continues to surround the institutionalized processes that create and maintain systemic oppression and privilege.

Unless meaningful connections are made across historically oppressed groups, and links are forged with privileged groups, meaningful change cannot occur. Coalition and ally building form the structural base for change. Without the collective action with supportive allies, oppressed people remain disempowered. The risk of division was recognized by Martin Niemoeller, who stated:

> In Germany, they came first for the Communists, and I didn't speak up because I wasn't a Communist. Then they came for the Jews, and I didn't speak up because I wasn't a Jew. Then they came for the trade unionists, and I didn't speak up because I wasn't a trade unionist. Then they came for the Catholics, and I didn't speak up because I was a Protestant. Then they came for me, and by that time no one was left to speak up. (qtd. in Bartlett, 1992, p. 684)

We no longer live in a world where we can exist in separate spheres. Bernice Johnson Reagon (2000) states,

> We've pretty much come to the end of a time when you can have a space that is "yours only"—just for the people you want to be there. . . . To a large extent it's because we have just finished with that kind of isolating. There is no hiding place. There is nowhere you can go and only be with people who are like you. It's over. Give it up. (p. 1105)

Questions for Consideration

1. Who are the oppressed groups in your country? What evidence is there that these group(s) are the marginalized?
2. Provide an example of the way oppression against a particular identity group is institutionalized in your country.
3. What is the economic and/or political impact of oppression on the oppressed group(s)?
4. Explore history in your country.
   a. Whose history is included in the history of your country?
   b. Whose history is not included in your country?
   c. Where would you locate accurate facts about these groups in order to tell the story from their perspective?
5. What stereotypes are assigned to the oppressed groups in your country?

CHAPTER 2

Critical Self-Reflection and Identity Development

Imagine that a map of the world is in front of you, could you put your finger on the spot that represented most closely the embodiment of who you are? How would you make your choice? Would it be determined by birth, ancestry, a sense of belonging?. . . What if after you weighed all the factors, thought carefully about what you liked and disliked, you could not put your finger down on one spot?

—Ackah, *Pan–Africanism*, 1999, n.p.

The unfinished character of human beings and the transformational character of reality necessitate that education be an ongoing activity. . . . The pursuit of full humanity, however, cannot be carried out in isolation or individualism, but only in fellowship and solidarity; therefore it cannot unfold in the antagonistic relations between oppressors and oppressed. No one can be authentically human while he [or she] prevents others from being so.

—Paulo Freire, *Pedagogy of the Oppressed*, 2000, pp. 84–85

It is perhaps an evolutionary strategy that humans tend to categorize their environment. Our brains do not focus on every detail in our environment and instead tend to "fill in" information to enable us to make quick decisions (Kokemail & de Lange, 2014; Perrinet & Bednar, 2015). Unfortunately, although it may enable us to navigate our daily lives, it may also result in making unconscious judgments about people based on their gender, ethnicity, color, and other social identities. This unconscious or implicit bias can cause us to act positively or negatively toward another person without much consideration about why we respond in this manner. The stereotypes we have learned about people of different ethnicities, gender, economic status, disabilities, accents, and color—that came from our parents, media, peers, and other sources—influence our unconscious reactions to others, even people we deem to be like us (Castelli, Zogmaister, & Tomelleri, 2009; Dasgupta, 2013; Mekawi, Bresin, & Hunter, 2015; Schofield, Deckman, Garris, DeWall, & Denson, 2015). These stereotypes and unconscious reactions keep us from recognizing our biases and their impact.

We enter this world lacking assumptions about other people. Through early socialization in the family, we begin to learn stereotypes, misinformation, myths, and partial histories that glorify some, vilify others, and erase still other people and events by making no mention of them at all. This misinformation is supported by institutional and cultural structures, such as the media, schools, religious institutions, government, and legal systems. As we grow, we consciously (or unconsciously) accept or reject what we have been taught in the past and what we are learning in the present (see Figure 2.1). What we accept becomes our "truth" and shapes how we see ourselves and others. When these "truths" are challenged, we can decide to maintain

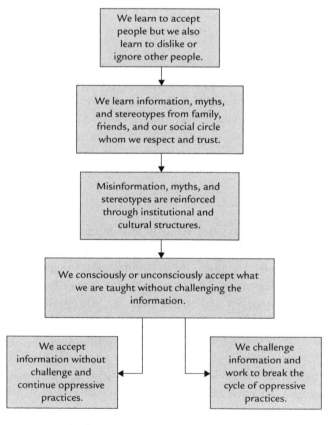

Figure 2.1: Learning and unlearning assumptions of hierarchical oppression.

our inaccurate beliefs and continue to act in ways that marginalize certain "other" people, or we can challenge information and work to break the cycle of oppressive practice and become allies with [other] marginalized groups.

Explicit biases are those we are aware of on a conscious level; implicit biases are those we have acquired but do not consciously recognize. It is easier to examine and reflect on our explicit biases. To recognize our implicit biases, it can be helpful to engage in critical self-reflection. Critical self-reflection, as part of ongoing learning and unlearning, can help us recognize our beliefs and assumptions and assess how they impact our behaviors and decisions. Engaging in this process can also help us see systems of institutionalized racism, sexism, classism, and heterosexism.

White supremacy is on the rise again in the United States and parts of Europe. Although white supremacy has a base of implicit bias, it is really grounded in explicit bias that accepts white privilege as correct. This privilege is considered a right that white supremacists deserve because they believe that they are intrinsically better than people of color. Acts of white supremacy range from covert and socially acceptable behavior (e.g., discrimination in housing, voting, employment) to overt and socially unacceptable behavior (e.g., slavery in the United States, apartheid in South Africa, the fascism of Nazi German, and the socially engineered white nation building in Australia). The criminal justice system in the United States, in which black and brown people are disproportionately arrested, convicted, and given longer sentences than whites for similar crimes, has been identified as the "new system of Jim Crow" (Alexander, 2012) and is a current example of white supremacy.

In the United States, there has been an increased interest in implicit bias and how it affects our behaviors. The country has watched as white police officers shoot unarmed black or brown suspects in case after case; the officers are usually not charged or are cleared of any wrongdoing. The examination of these interactions has suggested that officers, like the rest of us, may be reacting differently to suspects because of their implicit biases. This has led to increased study of how implicit bias can affect our interactions with others, even when we want to behave in a nondiscriminatory manner (Staats, Capatosto, Wright, & Jackson, 2016). Harvard's Race-Weapons Implicit Association Test reveals that people in the United States are more likely to shoot an unarmed person of color than an unarmed white person (see Project Implicit, n.d., for more information on the test). Fortunately, research suggests there are many ways we can mitigate the impact of implicit biases.

When people are viewed through a lens that reifies the customs, traditions, and values of the privileged group as "normal," people from "other" communities are judged negatively for not having the same customs, traditions, and values that have been defined as normal. This results in the marginalization of people who are not part of the privileged group. As a result, people from marginalized groups are viewed through a lens of deficit thinking and consequently are not seen for their strengths and encouraged to grow; rather, they are assumed to be less capable and left to languish (see Hatton & Smith, 1995, for discussion about reframing deficit thinking). After exploring our implicit biases, we are more likely to approach situations through nondeficit thinking, accepting that people have their own customs, traditions, and values that are neither more valuable, nor less valuable, than our own.

If we pause for a moment and contemplate who we are, we find that we have multiple social identities that are complex, multidimensional, and in flux. We each have identities of race/ethnicity/color/caste, gender, socioeconomic status, sexual orientation, religion, education, national origin, and ability/disability. As Tatum (2003) says, "Constructing our identities is a complex process for all of us, but for some it is more complicated than for others" (p. 167). Depending upon the context, one or more of our identities may provide us privilege or result in our oppression. Most of us reading this text have some identities that come with privilege and other identities that bring systemic mechanisms of oppression.

Engaging in critical multiculturalism and/or antioppression practice requires understanding the messages and power relationships between ourselves and others in a specific context (Keenan, 2004; Nagar, 2002). It also involves learning ways to reflexively examine who we are and our social location; our social identities, implicit biases, and privileges; and our experiences of oppression and marginalization. We propose that this first includes knowledge of identity development to help us understand our own. This knowledge can provide a base for critical self-reflection. Both identity development and critical self-reflection are discussed next.

IDENTITIES AND IDENTITY DEVELOPMENT

Social identity groups are not homogeneous but instead are "multifaceted, dynamic, complex and very heterogeneous" (Ferdman & Gallegos, 2001, p. 33). Each person is a unique blend of identities based on race, ethnicity, color, tribe, caste, nationality, gender, sexual orientation, ability-disability status, age, and more. Depending on context and location, one social identity may be more relevant than other identities held by an individual. Theorists often suggest that race is the master status—the status that is most important in determining how others respond to a person. Other theorists, however, suggest that, depending upon context, race may not be the most important identity. For example, in the Arab Gulf, nationality and citizenship are the master statuses that determine everything from employment options and salary to legally permitted marriage partners. Although people are more than a reflection of what other people imagine them to be, experiences do impact how individuals see themselves ethnically, racially, sexually, and so on.

Erik Erikson's (1968) stages of psychosocial development suggest that the challenge of adolescence is the development of identity versus role confusion. In Western, individualistic societies, independence is encouraged; this process of identity formation is conceptualized as an active exploration of one's identity(ies) until "commitment" to a set of roles and ideologies is achieved (Erikson, 1968). Developing a positive ethnic identity is considered as important for an overall healthy, integrated, cohesive identity (e.g., Chavous et al., 2003; Schwartz, Zamboanga, Weisskirch, & Rodriguez, 2009; Smith & Silva, 2011). A healthy, cohesive identity can mediate the effects of discrimination (Greene, Way, & Pahl, 2006). On the other hand, some theorists are critical of identity theories, noting, "For all the talk about the social construction of knowledge, identity politics de facto seems to slide towards the premise that social groups have essential identities" (Girlin, 1994, p. 153).

It is important to note that the stage theories of identity development come primarily from Western perspectives and research. Although these models have been applied in non-Western contexts (see Schwartz, Zamboanga, Meca, & Ritchie, 2012), it is unclear if they are appropriate in all non-Western contexts. For example, "cultures that are rooted in collectivism and interdependence may promote a different route to identity formation that emphasizes accepting and embracing one's social and familial roles" (Cheng & Berman, 2012, p. 117). In collectivist societies, healthy identity development is not about reaching a state of "autonomous self" but about creating a healthy identity in relationship with others (Lam, 1997). Therefore, as currently iterated, most stage models of identity development are not necessarily universal or readily applicable to adolescents and emerging adults from other cultural contexts (Berman, You, Schwartz, Teo, & Mochizuki, 2011).

To become aware of one's own privileges and oppression, a critical understanding of identity development models is considered helpful. These theories suggest various "stages" individuals move through to develop a healthy identity (Cross 1978, 1991; Ferdman & Gallegos, 2001; Helms, 1993c; Tatum, 2003), although not necessarily in a linear manner. To this, ecological models add recognition of the sociocultural factors that affect the way identity is integrated into one's personality, such as (a) parents, family, peers, schools, religious organizations, and the media; (b) systemic factors, such as socio-economic class, discrimination, and quality of interracial interactions; and (c) physical and personal attributes (Helms, 1993a). Wijeyesinghe notes the influence of racial ancestry, cultural attachment, early experience and socialization, political awareness and orientation, spirituality, other social identities, social and historical context, and physical appearance (2012). Others identify history, family, and cultural factors (Sue & Sue, 1993).

Chestang (1972, 1984) offers additional factors to consider around the development of racial identities in a hostile environment. When people experience social inconsistency in combination with social injustice, the result may be personal impotence. People who are marginalized and oppressed often feel hopeless because rules are applied inconsistently based on a person's privilege. Consequently, one of two responses emerges, the depreciated or the transcendent character. The depreciated character accepts things as they are and works within the system, accepting the status quo. Transcendent characters, however, do not accept the status quo and make every effort to change the system regardless of the consequences. The struggle against abuse, the presence of tolerance and restraint, and the need to persevere affect the development of racial identity and group identification.

Identity development is neither static nor linear. Theories of racial/ ethnoracial identity development have been a topic of interest for several decades. Research has shown that the exploration of racial identity can be positively correlated with well-being (Syed et al., 2013). Not everyone starts at the same place, nor does everyone progress in a step-by-step manner. The manner in which one chooses identities to integrate into one's personality depends on sociocultural and systemic factors, along with personal attributes (Helms, 1993a).

Racial Identity Development Models

William E. Cross and Janet Helms first introduced a stage model of racial identity development (Cross, 1978, 1980, 1991) that was later expanded by Helms (1984, 1993c, 1994). Stage models outline a path that people may take in developing a healthy racial identity. Models of racial identity development include, but are not limited to, African American racial identity development (Cross, 1978, 1991; Helms, 1993c, 1994), biracial identity development (Miville, 2005; Miville, Constantine, Baysden, & So-Lloyd, 2005), multiracial identity development (Kich, 1992; Poston, 1990; Root, 2003), white racial identity development (Helms, 1993d), African identity development (Ndubuisi, 2013), Asian and Asian American identity

Table 2.1: AFRICAN AMERICAN AND WHITE RACIAL MODELS OF IDENTITY DEVELOPMENT

African American Racial Identity Development	White Racial Identity Development
1. **Pre-encounter:** Internalized the beliefs and values of the dominant culture. May de-emphasize their own racial membership. Unaware of racial identification.	1. **Contact**: Does not acknowledge racial differences and does not see racism as an issue.
2. **Encounter**: Through repeated experiences or events begins to realize that African American racial identity matters.	2. **Disintegration**: Begins to accept that there are racial differences but ambivalent about the reasons. Very conflicted about the cause.
3. **Immersion/Emersion:** Embraces and studies black identity and black culture, excluding all other racial identities. Develops a stronger affinity for embracing black history and black culture.	3. **Reintegration**: Those who still struggle in the previous stage often mollify themselves by "blaming the victim." They acknowledge that whites are privileged but because they are more deserving.
4. **Internalization**: Ones positive racial identity becomes a critical element of the whole person. Can engage in discussions about race without taking a defensive position. Can engage in meaningful relationships with white people without feeling they have compromised their own identity.	4. **Pseudo-independence**: They no longer believe that whites inherently deserve privilege, but they turn to blacks instead of themselves to uncover and confront racism. The journey continues in embracing how they can be white and nonracist.
5. **Internalization-commitment:** Has a strong race identity and serves as an advocate to teach others about African American culture.	5. **Immersion/Emersion:** Actively engages in embracing their own white identity and both positive and negative historical actions. They commit to being antiracist. Also committed to reaching out to other people who are struggling with white identity issues.
	6. **Autonomy:** Has a clear and positive understanding of their white identity and the implications of privilege. Actively engages in social justice causes.

development (Kim, 2001; Lam, 1997), and Latino/Latina[1] identity development (Ferdman & Gallegos, 2011). Although we include "white racial identity" development theory here, "whiteness" is not an ethnicity or nationality but instead "a form of power" (Olson, 2004, p. 113), one that undergirded colonialism around the globe. Models of African American racial identity development and white racial identity development are presented in Table 2.1.

1. "Latina/o" is often used interchangeably with "Hispanic," although "Latina/o" refers specifically to people from Latin America and "Hispanic" refers to people with origins in Spanish-speaking countries. Latinx is increasingly used as a gender neutral replacement for Latino/Latina.

African American Racial Identity Development

The model of racial identity development for people who are African American, first introduced by Cross (1978, 1980, 1991) and expanded by Helms (1984, 1993c, 1994), outlines the path that people who are African American may take in developing a healthy racial identity. Helms's (1993c) amended model, which focuses on worldview, delineates the five stages of racial identity formation: pre-encounter, encounter, immersion/emersion, internalization, and internalization/commitment.

During the pre-encounter stage, people who are African American idealize the worldview of the dominant white culture and are unaware of African American and black cultures. It is assumed that people who are white create the status quo through their extraordinary efforts. Other African Americans are devalued and not seen as good role models; therefore, success or failure is attributed to how well the traits associated with whiteness are imitated (Helms, 1993b). The person is unaware of their racial identity and identifies with the dominate culture.

During the encounter stage, the person becomes aware that race is the delineator that determines or influences life options. A single event or an accumulation of events may lead to the realization that the dominant worldview does not value the person's ethnicity. During the struggle to learn one's identity, a person often vacillates between shedding the pre-encounter identity and accepting a not yet clearly articulated African American identity. This phase is wrought with mixed emotions, ranging from confusion in the earlier part of this stage to euphoria later in the stage.

The immersion/emersion stage consists of two phases. First is the existence of a positive authentic African American identity and a black or African-centric worldview. The individual adopts an African American identity and abandons the dominate-culture identity. The person might also overtly express a blackness that conforms to white stereotypes of blackness. During this part, African Americans may express anger toward people who are white. Whites are viewed as oppressors due to unequal treatment and the bias African Americans experience; anger might also be focused toward other African Americans who do not share their new perspective. The individual experiences emotional ups and downs in trying to come to terms with a new identity and worldview. Immersion is a process of self-exploration, whereas emersion is a process of acceptance and proud expression of African American culture, customs, and values. Emersion offers the possibility of escape from immersion. During emersion, the person accepts the new identity, withdrawing into a supportive African

American community where they can engage in cathartic experiences. During this phase, a person may engage in a range of social or political activities that allow exploration of African American and African identity. The emersion into African American culture allows the person to develop a nonstereotypical African American worldview.

Finally, the internalization/commitment stage marks the continuation and nurturing of positive African American identity and involvement in social and civic activities; it involves teaching and challenging others who deny African American culture. The internalization/commitment stage marks the point at which a person positively integrates the unique elements of one's personal identity with one's African American identity. The person can now face the world from a position of strength and identifies with the African American community. The person rejects racism and other forms of oppression, not only of African Americans but also other vulnerable and marginalized groups; and the person can have positive relationships with allies who are white.

White Racial Identity Development

White people who fail to see themselves as racialized—that is, they tend not to think of themselves in racial terms, even though they think of people who are not white in racial terms—also fail to see the ways in which they are privileged. People who are white know that they are white, but this is often translated into nationality, such as being European, Australian, Canadian, or American, rather than a racial identity. They do not have any experience of understanding race and how it shapes their lives. They typically do not think about their whiteness, nor do they think about the privilege bestowed on them because of their skin color. Far and away the most troublesome consequence of this race obliviousness is the failure to recognize the privileges society confers upon them simply because they have white skin. The privilege of white skin provides a set of advantages one receives simply by being born with features that society values (Dalton, 2002). The benefits of white skin privilege are far ranging. One of the consequences is being confident that they will not be discriminated against because of their skin color in a job interview or when they try to rent an apartment. It also involves things like seeing people of their own race represented on television.

This inability or unwillingness to think of themselves in racial terms produces huge blind spots. It leaves people who are white baffled by the amount of energy people of color pour into questions of racial identity. It makes it difficult for people who are white to understand why many people of color have a sense of group consciousness that influences the choices they make as individuals. It blinds them to the fact that their lives are shaped by race just as much as the lives of people of color. How people who are considered white view life's possibilities, whom they regard as heroes, the extent to which they feel a particular country is rightfully theirs, and the extent to which that belief is reinforced by society—all of this, and more, is a function of race. The internalized assumption of normality prevents them from imagining other possibilities.

Skin color is a complex social indicator that promotes differential power and privilege between people who are seen as white and those who are considered people of color (Pinderhughes, 1989). One's perception of reality is seldom questioned, except when one encounters others who are different and/or have differing worldviews. These encounters offer people who are white the opportunity to develop knowledge and awareness of themselves as racial beings. People who are white are generally unaware of ways to develop a racial identity and have few opportunities to understand what it means to be white until they choose to embrace nonracist perspectives (Carter, 1995). White identity theory explores a developmental process that people who are white may engage in to gain a better understanding of themselves and the environments in which they live.

Helms's (1993d) white racial identity development theory, called the abandonment of racism, runs parallel to the African American racial identity development model and consists of six stages (as presented in Table 2.1) that occur in two phases. The process begins with the "abandonment-of-racism phase," which has three stages: contact, disintegration, and reintegration. This is followed by the "defining-a-nonracist-white-identity phase," which also involves three stages: pseudo-independence, immersion/emersion, and autonomy.

In the contact stage, people who are white develop a vague awareness of the presence of people of color. During this stage, people who are white may approach people of color with a tentative curiosity and may have only a vague or superficial awareness of their own whiteness. At this stage, they still use their own whiteness as the norm against which they compare people of color, unaware that there are multiple ways to evaluate others. They pass judgment without recognizing that whiteness is the norm against which they evaluate the physical appearance, customs, values, and behavior of all others. Their interactions with people of color in social and occupational settings are limited, which means they have little opportunity to test their assumptions about people of color.

During the disintegration stage, people who are white start to develop a consciousness of whiteness, although it is often conflicted due to a vague awareness of inequality, resulting in guilt and confusion. At this point people who are white are not ready to acknowledge the extent and impact of their whiteness. To reduce uncomfortable feelings, people who are white may avoid people of color and/or attempt to minimize or deny the existence of racism.

During reintegration, the third stage of phase 1, people acknowledge their white identity but believe that the social structures that privilege them and disadvantage others are part of a natural order. Similarities that they observe between people who are white and people of color are minimized or denied. People can easily remain at this stage, engaging in racist behavior until some insight causes them to question this stance.

During pseudo-independence, the first stage of the second phase, the individual begins the formation of a positive white identity, engaging in an intellectual process in an effort to make sense of what they have learned. Assumptions, including notions of superiority and inferiority based on race, are questioned in earnest. The person begins to intellectually acknowledge that they have a responsibility to help dismantle systems that oppress people of color. Yet people at this stage may still behave in ways that inadvertently maintain the status quo. They may now see people of color as victims but may also believe that the solution to the problem is to help people of color adopt the culture of the white dominant society. They do not yet see that ethnoracial differences in values, perspectives, and behaviors are viable alternative ways of being. They still measure all people against the white ideal. During this stage, the motives of individuals who are earnest about developing a positive white racial identity may be questioned by the racial groups they are trying to champion. They may also be viewed with suspicion by family members or other people they know who are white. Those who continue the campaign against race-based social injustice are well on their way to developing a racial identity that no longer privileges whiteness and marginalizes people of color.

Immersion/emersion is the stage during which people acquire a strong commitment to the development of a positive white racial identity, and to replacing myths and stereotypes about whiteness and people of color with accurate information. The questions that are asked at this stage are "Who am I racially/ethically?" "Who do I want to be?" and "Who are you really?" People often facilitate this journey by reading about others who are white who have engaged in racial identity struggles. They may also participate in white consciousness-raising groups that are committed to addressing racial injustice. At this stage, individuals no longer see people of color as needing to be fixed. They fully accept the need for people who are white to play an integral role in the change process.

Autonomy, the final stage, describes the internalization of a new definition of whiteness and a commitment to nurture this identity. The person is now committed to eliminating oppressive behaviors and no longer villifies or pays tribute to others based on their identity group membership. While developing an autonomous identity, the person also seeks out opportunities to engage with members of other racial, ethnic, and cultural identity groups. This final stage of white racial identity does not represent the end of racial identity development, but a new beginning that must be nurtured, encouraged, and respected. This stage marks the individual's acceptance that this is an ongoing process requiring openness to new information and different worldviews. Tatum (1994) describes the final stage as much like a spiral staircase that allows the individual to revisit previous stages before moving forward. As in the final stage in African American racial identity development, the person no longer feels the need to pass judgment on others based on identity group membership.

Biracial/Multiracial Identity Development

Poston (1990) developed one of the first biracial identity development models. According to Poston, biracial identity development occurs over five stages: personal identity, choice of group categorization, enmeshment/denial, appreciation, and integration. Although Poston and Root both recognized the role of institutionalized racism on identity development, Root (2003) disputed Poston's stage model and proposed a strategy model for multiracial people based on a combination of personal and environmental factors. Within this model, five identity outcomes are possible, including assigned (identification with the race assigned to a person), mixed (identification with more than one race), single group (identification with one of their racial identities), new racial group (identification with a new racial group), and white. Likewise, the Continuum of Biracial Identity (COBI) considers multiple ways multiracial people can identify (Rochquemore & Laszloffy, 2005). Within this model people who are biracial may identify at any point along a continuum: from a single identity (identity 1), to a blended identity, to single identity (identity 2)—a blended identity may favor a single identity or maintain a biracial focus. These exemplars move away from stage models toward ecological models.

People who are multiracial are influenced by complex interactions of power and identity (Wijeyesinghe, 2012). As their identities intersect, they may experience both privilege, if one of their identities is white, and marginalization based on other identities. Multiracial people may further "reflect an integration of racial and nonracial social identities, such as gender, ethnicity, sexual orientation, and socioeconomic class" (Wijeyesinghe, 2012, p. 90). Current concerns may take precedence over racial identity. For instance, someone who is gay may find that identity more salient in their social and geographic context. Perceptions and appearance may also have an impact if, for instance, a person identifies as Latina while those in her work context see her as black.

Under the Factor Model of Multiracial Identity (FMMI) (Wijeyesinghe, 2001), multiple factors are recognized as impacting racial identity; this model goes beyond an assumption that there is a right or wrong choice of identity. Further integration takes place in the Intersectional Model of Multiracial Identity (IMMI) (Wijeyesinghe, 2012). Within these models, the interaction between race and other identities is respected and the fluidity across identities is acknowledged. The ecological approach to multiracial identity goes even further by recognizing the impact of geography and region as increasingly important in a global world (Wijeyesinghe, 2012). Someone raised in a multiracial region such as Hawaii may have a very different experience and identity than someone raised in a community where there are few multiracial people.

Transgender Identity Development

Both stage and lifespan models have been developed to describe nonconforming gender identity development (e.g., transgender, bigender, and queergender)—the sense of one's gender as different from one's assigned biological sex (Brockting, 2013; Brockting & Coleman, 2007). The stigma, discrimination, and violence often experienced by people with a nonconforming gender identity have been noted to affect identity development (Brockting, 2013). Fortunately, connection to the trans community has been linked to resilience (Testa, Jimenez, & Rankin, 2013). For example, before a person identifies as transgender, research suggests that knowing someone and/or interacting with someone who is transgender reduces fear and suicidality, and increases comfort with the identity (Testa et al., 2013).

Researchers suggest that trans people typically go through a four- (Pardo, 2008) or five-stage process to transgender identity, similar to sexual orientation identity development stage models (Brockting & Coleman, 2007). The stages include (a) pre–coming out when the person experiences feeling different, (b) exploration of gender identity, (c) coming out, (d) engaging in an intimate relationship, and (e) identity resolution or integration. Most trans people have feelings of *being different* from early childhood (*pre–coming out*). This is often manifested starting from age 3, and as late as age 12, as feeling that something is "out of sync between the body and mind" (Pardo, 2008, p. 2). Puberty brings unwanted and confusing body changes, resulting in a period of *exploration* "as the person seeks to develop a sense of true self while balancing feelings of guilt and shame, pressures to conform, and the need for secrecy" (Pardo, 2008, p. 2). Exploration of gender identity often includes exploration of sexuality and appearance.

Successful *coming out/disclosure* (acceptance from others) is positively correlated with positive identity. As part of disclosure, trans people may begin to modify their public persona. This may involve name changes, use of different pronouns, clothes acceptable to their identified gender, and sometimes body modification. During this time, some trans people immerse themselves in the lesbian, gay, bisexual, and transgender (LGBT) or trans communities (Grossman & D'Augelli, 2006; Pardo, 2008). In Brockting's model, the additional stage of *intimacy* occurs when the person engages in their first intimate relationship as the gender with which they identify. A positive trans *identity resolution* or *integration* is complete when the "individual achieves a stable, healthy sense of self" (Pardo, 2008, p. 2).

Brockting's (2013) lifespan model identifies the challenges a person may experience during childhood, adolescence, adulthood, and later life. In childhood, a person is often already aware that they "feel different." Supportive environments allow for gender ambiguity while the child explores their sense of gender identity. Only about 25% of children with a nonconforming gender identity carry that identity into adolescence (Brockting, 2013). Like their peers, adolescence is a time for gender-nonconforming children to explore their identities, including sexuality. Puberty can bring distress as the body develops sex characteristics that are inconsistent with a person's sense of self (Brockting, 2013). Negative reactions of parents to a gender-nonconforming child are correlated with suicide attempts (Grossman & D'Augelli, 2006).

There is no single way of experiencing adulthood as a gender-nonconforming person. Although the majority of adolescents who are gender nonconforming continue to identify as such in adulthood, there are many trajectories (Brockting, 2013). For example, some gender-nonconforming adults get married, have children, and try to conceal or contain their gender identity. Other gender-nonconforming adults may make changes to their gender roles and expression and/or make modifications to their body to bring consistency to their sense of gender. The process of transgender identity development continues throughout their life. Elders who may have delayed coming out to avoid discrimination may now feel able to disclose their identity. Ideally, a person comes to embrace "an identity that transcends the gender dichotomy of male versus female" (Brockting, 2013, p. 748).

Emerging Models of Identity Development

Multidimensional models are emerging, providing new perspectives. Sue and Sue (2016) present stage models of racial identity development expanded through a sociopolitical lens. Wijeyesinghe (2012) expands her previous work, intersecting multicultural identity theories with views on social identity; and Renn (2012) connects psychological, sociological, and ecological views with racial identity development. Wijeyesinghe and Jackson (2012) review emerging models that blend the stage models with ecological and sociological theories. Seller, Smith, Shelton, Rowley, and Chavous (1998) developed a multidimensional racial identity model synthesizing the key components of universal models with those that recognize unique individual and cultural dimensions for African Americans.

Holvino's (2012) model of simultaneity examines the impact of globalization. The ecological context has expanded due to the international flow of goods, capital, and labor. People are crossing borders physically and virtually, impacting cultures. The increase in immigration (including the flow of refugees and asylum seekers) is shifting relationships and assumptions. The movement of people across cultural borders reforms identity. Political and intellectual forces also impact identity, which "is constructed through language and the social practices of communities" (Holvino, 2012, p. 162). As Holvino states,

> As a Puerto Rican scholar and practitioner based in the United States and working internationally I welcome these changes. As a Latina, one-dimensional models of identity have not served me well. For example, when I am given the choice to sit with the women's caucus (my gender identity) or with the Hispanics' caucus (my racial-ethnic identity) I am torn as I cannot separate these aspects of my identity that are inseparable. (Holvino, 2006, as cited in Holvino, 2012, p. 162)

The model of simultaneity has the potential "to engage with the multiplicity and complexity of identities in today's globalized world" (Holvino, 2012, p. 163). Examining existing theories of racial identity from "an intersectional lens holds the promise of uncovering new insights from models that may be years or even decades old" (Wijeyesinghe, 2012, p. 101). The model of simultaneity pulls from and adds to transnational feminism and intersectionality. (Transnational feminism is reviewed in Chapter 4, and intersectionality is the focus of Chapter 6.)

INTERCULTURAL AWARENESS AND SENSITIVITY

Another level of reflection and knowledge building involves building cultural awareness and developing cultural sensitivity. Bennett and Bennett (2004) envisioned a model for assessing awareness of and sensitivity to differences. Over time, the Intercultural Development Continuum (IDC) was developed. The IDC offers a framework for understanding the process of multicultural learning (Hammer, 2012). The phases of African American racial identity development and white racial identity development fit across the IDC.

The IDC is a continuum that moves from a monocultural mindset through transitional orientations to intercultural/global mindsets (see the continuum at https://idiinventory.com/products/the-intercultural-development-continuum-idc/). The markers along the continuum move from *denial* to *polarization* to *minimization* to *acceptance* to *adaptation*.

1. Denial does not see and is not interested in cultural diversity.
2. Polarization sees others through their own lens—denigrating and judging others, finding difference threatening. People may view their own culture as normal and superior; or they may see other cultures as perfect and their own as inferior.
3. Minimization has some awareness of difference but downplays those differences. It looks at difference through a lens of commonality. At this stage, however, they still consider their own culture as a central point of reference for interpreting all cultures. They may even view their culture as superior.
4. Acceptance recognizes and explores differences. It is curious, interested, and able to explore the complexity of differences, but it is not yet sure how to incorporate this information.
5. Adaptation is the point when people are able to shift perspectives and adapt to cultural context. Within this phase, the possibility increases for shifting cultural perspectives and bridging difference.

As a continuum, the IDC allows us to picture a flow across time and context, highlighting potential points of intervention toward change. Denial and polarization reflect early stages of intercultural identity development. Once minimization is reached, the possibility increases for building a relationship of trust. As one works through this with safety and respect, they can take steps toward increasing their consciousness of difference. Movement into acceptance is where one encounters, disintegrates, and reintegrates culture, identity, and difference. It is with adaptation (internalization/commitment) that bridging and activism are possible. This is the beginning of an ongoing process.

The Intercultural Development Inventory (IDI) is an instrument that can be used to measure developmental phases (Intercultural Development Inventory, n.d.). The IDI measures where people think they are developmentally and also where they are currently. People often think they are farther along on the continuum than the inventory indicates. The instrument is valid, reliable, and generalizable across cultures; it has been used across the globe (Hammer, 2011; IDI, n.d.).

Knowing where an individual or group is on the IDC can aid in designing a change model, whether for individuals, organizations, community groups, or educational systems. Even at the adaptation phase, growth continues. Just as the final phase of white racial identity is the beginning of identity development, not the end, adaptation within the IDC is not the end of learning and developing; it is the beginning of an ongoing process.

Learning can begin with self-reflection and a process of exposure to multiple cultures. Intercultural learning opportunities can start with exploration through books, theatre, and the arts. Learning also can be more interactive, involving classes, community activities, workshops, interpersonal interactions, and travel. Reflective writing across the exploration process supports knowledge building and internal growth. Engaging in study abroad opportunities, combined with self-reflection, provides the opportunity for unique and meaningful change.

CRITICAL SELF-REFLECTION

A critical multicultural perspective requires one to evaluate how one's own beliefs, values, and perspectives may or may not contribute to biases or discrimination against people from other identity groups. The goal of self-reflection in critical multiculturalism is to develop an awareness of one's own identities and increase one's awareness of systemic social structures of oppression as a foundation for activism. Critical self-reflection facilitates this exploration of one's values, attitudes, and personal history, which can encourage ownership of, and deepen responsibility for, learning. Examining one's own biases and prejudicial attitudes, particularly when one is learning about and working with different identity groups, can facilitate a process of change (Croskerry, Singhal, & Mamede, 2013).

Although change begins within oneself, it does not occur in isolation. It can only occur in relation to others. As Bambara (1981) asserts in *This Bridge Called My Back*, "We have got to know each other better and teach each other our ways, our views, if we're to remove the scales . . . and get the work done" (p. vii). The way people see the world (worldview) is socially constructed within the context of the social systems and identities in which they live. When people do not know each other, they are able to build the "delusion" that everyone is like us and/or our way of thinking, our beliefs, worldview, and values are "normal" and correct. Within this context, we become ethnocentric, judging others by our views and standards.

It is difficult to engage in objective reflection about oneself. The very concept of self-awareness is socially constructed (Gergen, 2011), which brings the process of attempting to engage in self-awareness full circle and illustrates the difficulty of grasping the concept. Kondrat (1999) identifies three types of self-reflection: reflective self-awareness, reflexive self-awareness, and critical reflectivity. The distinct meanings of these three terms are still under debate with *reflective self-awareness, reflexive self-awareness*, and *critical reflectivity* often used interchangeably (D'Cruz, Gillingham, & Melendez, 2015). In this book, the definition of these three terms is as follows:

> **Reflective self-awareness (or self-awareness reflection).** One examines oneself to realistically assess one's own biases, "knowledge, values, qualities, skills and behaviours" (Henrique, 2016, n.p.). Reflection is about looking back on past experiences as a way of understanding one's self and the world (Kondrat, 1999).
>
> **Reflexive self-awareness**. This involves the ability to notice why things are the way they are, specifically one's part in it. It is about noticing patterns and asking how one's own worldview, values, socialization, ideology, biases, and assumptions create one's reality. "What we know and how we know become the foci of scrutiny, along with an awareness of how relations of power are complicit in knowledge creation" (D'Cruz et al., 2015, p. 78).
>
> **Critical reflectivity**. The goal of critical reflectivity is for individuals to become aware of "the sociohistorical reality which shapes their lives and of their capacity to transform that reality" (Freire, 1970, quoted by Kondrat, 1999, p. 472). Critical reflection has an "emancipatory element" as it provides people with the "capacity to question and

change existing power relations" (Fook, 1999, pp. 201–202, citing Brookfield, 1995).

When we consider the possibility that there may be alternative interpretations of reality, we allow ourselves to explore the significance and impact of our interactions with others. Assessing how we perceive and interact with people who are different from ourselves is a meaningful way to identify unconscious or implicit biases.

Advocates of critical reflectivity start with the supposition that all people and institutions somehow contribute to the oppressive behaviors and practices that perpetuate inequality (Kondrat, 1999). This suggests that one's daily interactions with others, whether conscious or unconscious, intentional or not, have broad and profound ramifications regarding racism, sexism, heterosexism, nationalism, and ableism. Because one cannot wholly escape societal influences, one's conscious antiracist convictions, attitudes, and behaviors do not exclude one from participation in the perpetuation of inequality. Racism and other oppressive acts are often perceived as overt actions, but inaction can produce the same results. What we do not know or are not conscious of can have unintended negative consequences for marginalized people.

Although identity development and cultural sensitivity models outline the phases for developing a nonracist white identity, they do not provide guidance on how to do this (Helms, 2015). Sue (2003) developed guidelines for the development of a nonracist white identity. It is the responsibility of people who are white to do their own work to learn about the identity group with which they want to be an ally; it is not the responsibility of people of color or other marginalized groups to teach those with privilege. As noted,

> our goal cannot be to bring in people of color and expect that they will school us. Organizers of color have enough work already. In our pursuit to get educated, we need to go to more events and actions organized by people of color and show support, listen, and learn. We need to read the amazing writers that are out there. We can pay attention to how the system works (when we are in jail, in court, in classrooms, at work, and on the street). (Crass, n.d.)

Obviously, when offered or it is available, take the opportunity to learn from healthy and strong members of the identity group for which one wants to be an ally. Find opportunities to learn experientially, monitor biases and fears, and commit to action in opposition to racism. See Box 2.1 as a student struggles with these issues.

Box 2.1
A STUDENT'S STRUGGLE WITH WHITE SUPREMACY AND IMPLICIT BIAS

As I received the assignment, I knew it was going to be very interesting for both my family and myself. Our professor asked us to interview the oldest member of our family to determine how the family developed beliefs and attitudes about individuals and groups of people. The professor provided a list of questions for us to ask:

1. What are your views about race/ethnic/tribal/caste relations in the twenty-first century?
2. Did you have friends from other races/ethnicities/tribes/castes as a child and young adult? Do you now have friends of another race/ethnicity/tribe/caste?
3. When did you first become aware of race/ethnicity/tribes/castes?
4. What messages about race/ethnicity/tribes/castes did you receive from your family and community as a child?
5. How would your family feel if you were to marry someone from a different race/ethnicity/tribe/caste?

I knew this would be an interesting assignment because, as a white Afrikaner in postapartheid South Africa, I was involved in a relationship with a Zulu man, and no one in my family knew about this relationship. Frankly, I was afraid to tell anyone. I sat at the dinner table at home too many times and listened to numerous family debates about different racial/ethnic/tribal/castes groups in our society. Early on in my life I had received a message that no one in our family should marry anyone outside our race/ethnicity/tribe/caste.

I decided to make this assignment even more interesting by asking my boyfriend (whom I am considering marrying) to do the same with his family. I later realized that I was subconsciously trying to ease my guilt. I was hoping that my boyfriend's family was as close minded as mine. The taboo subject that we never explored as a couple was why I had not invited him home. I had, however, been to his home on several occasions. His family asked me numerous questions about my family, but they remained silent on a significant question: Did my parents know that I was in an interracial relationship?

What my grandmother said during the interview was that "we should love everyone and people are people and we should treat everyone the same." She went on to say that she really did not know any "black people." She said she learned about their existence when her family first moved to Durban, and she mentioned to her mom how tan they were and wondered aloud if she could get that type of tan. My grandmother still remembers her mother's response and the fear in her mother's eyes; the message was "They are bad people, never talk to one, and never let them in your home because they will hurt you." My grandmother clearly had received cultural messages from her parents that gave her negative beliefs about people of color. She never questioned why they felt this way; she just passed these negative feelings down to her children, including my mother. My grandmother obeyed her parents, and from that moment on she never approached anyone who was black. What she learned on her own about this group of people came from the media, and that information was mostly negative because of institutional racism. In her mind, black people who succeeded got away from the "bad blacks" and assimilated into the dominant culture.

When I asked her what would happen if I married a black man, she looked me in the eye and said that she knew I would never do something like that. I was her beautiful granddaughter, and I was going to marry someone like us and have many children. I did not want to disillusion and hurt my grandmother. I too had to be honest: I had not told her because I did not want to face my family's disapproval. At that point, I told her that I had a black boyfriend and I was considering marrying him. My grandmother first thought I was joking. When she realized I was being honest, she sat in silence for a few moments. Finally, she shook her head and said that I was being selfish. I was not thinking about our family or the fact that if we had children, they would have a hard life. She told me I should look for someone of my "own kind." This was one of the code phrases from the list that my professor gave us entitled "When You Know You Have Met a Bigot."

I could not believe that my grandmother, whom I loved so much, was a bigot. She did not ask me if I was happy or if I loved this man; she just wanted me to get over it. Instead of being angry at her, I realized that, despite the turmoil of apartheid and the current situation in South Africa, our family had never talked openly about the issue of race and how it had affected us. I told my mom about my relationship and the conversation I had with her mother. She listened but she also did not encourage my relationship. I was really angry at my mom. I shouted that she taught her children to treat all people the same. All through our childhood she had insisted that our family was accepting of others. She marched us to church each Sunday and sent us to Catholic school for 12 years, and the message was always the same: "Love thy neighbor." It was a commandment from God. "Are we hypocrites?" was the final question that I asked her.

What I learned from this assignment is not a surprise. My family is very bigoted. Once "the race elephant in the room" was discussed openly, I discovered the biggest surprise of all: I was a passive racist. I realized that I was liberal regarding race as long as black people thought like me.

I now must admit I was just tolerant of black people and ignored the fact that I needed to change and become more self-aware and open in order to explore racial differences. I should have been open about my interracial relationship and willing to question my family values. I should have challenged my family to consider why we are racist.

I now understand why people who are black do not trust people who are white. These days, most people who are white are conditioned to say the politically correct thing but are really afraid to explore why racism exists. We must grapple with the impact of unexamined privilege. Are we ever going to demand social justice for all people?

I am in a relationship that I should have shared with my family. I should have discussed with them the ups and downs of loving someone who is different. I kept this secret to myself. I knew all along that my family would not be supportive when I shared my news. I am disappointed in them, but I am even more deeply disappointed in myself.

This assignment also helped me understand Janet Helms's white identity model. I was so naive, and I have a lot of personal work to do to dispel my beliefs about other groups of people. I love my boyfriend. I now have questions, and I have made a commitment to address them. I am on what will be a lifelong quest to understand the complex issues of racism. My boyfriend and I have committed to work hard as a couple, not hiding from the issues concerning race that we confront in our relationship.

As a person who is entering a helping profession, I must embrace a commitment to becoming more aware of why I do the things that I do. This is critical if I wish to help others. I hate what I found out about myself and my family, but what would have happened if I had never discovered this? If I had failed to do this, how could I work with people from different cultural backgrounds?

Previously, as I sat in class and heard black students telling their stories, I dismissed those stories by telling myself it was not my fault; I did not do anything to contribute to the plight of black Africans—I was not part of apartheid. Thinking honestly about this is difficult. I understand why students who are white are reluctant to speak up; it is hard to process these things. It is time, however, that we do so if we want to develop the skills necessary to create more inclusive communities by truly examining these "isms."

This student used an assignment for critical self-reflection. She not only explored identity conflicts but also her explicit and implicit biases. What she and her family do not acknowledge is the assumption of white supremacy.

Critical reflectivity exercises may help people recognize behaviors and attitudes that contribute to many "isms" (e.g., racism, sexism, heterosexism, nationalism). Unfortunately, it can be difficult to recognize one's own biases; it may be easier to recognize biases in others. An approach that encompasses both oneself and the sociopolitical context breaks this gridlock. The following questions, developed by Kondrat (1999), reflect the spirit of critical reflectivity.

1. What do I do on a day-to-day basis that might contribute to inequality?
2. What have I learned about how to perceive or how to relate to members of my own identity group(s) or other groups, and what is the source of that learning?
3. What do I know about how to relate to and interpret the behavior of others who occupy social locations (i.e., class, gender, ethnoracial identity, sexual orientation, ability, religion, nationality) that are similar to, as well as different from, my own?
4. What have I learned about how to interpret the behavior of people whose ethnoracial, sexual orientation, ability, nationality, or religion is different from my own? What if I add class and gender/sex to the equation?
5. What do I know about my conscious intentions when I interact with someone who is African, Latino/Latina, indigenous, Asian, Arabic, Australian, European, biracial or multiracial; an expatriate, a refugee or asylum seeker, or an immigrant; people who are gay, lesbian, bisexual, transgender, or intersex; and people with disabilities?
6. Why do the consequences or outcomes of my actions not fit with or match my good intentions? (Kondrat, 1999)

Failure to recognize personal biases or negative attitudes toward others results in resistance to owning the possibility that one may be racist, sexist, or heterosexist (Kondrat, 1999). When a person examines their personal attitudes and behaviors in isolation from the larger social, political, and economic context, the structural barriers that impede access to resources are not acknowledged. Neither the distortions of history nor the social construction of meaning is evaluated. This often leads to racist acts and other oppressive practices. Individuals can fail to assess their own racist or biased thoughts and behaviors, as well as those of the community (see Box 2.2). Or they might acknowledge that biases exist but feel that there is nothing they can do to change these situations (Kondrat, 1999).

Engaging in critical self-reflection offers an opportunity for the assessment of personal beliefs, intentions, and attitudes. The process highlights areas in which assumptions and interactions between oneself and others result in behaviors that perpetuate the oppression of people who

Box 2.2

REFLECTIONS OF A COMMUNITY AGENCY INTERN

Natasia, a heterosexual, white intern in her mid-twenties, is completing her practicum in a nongovernmental (NGO) community organization. She has been assigned several cases throughout the academic year. As she approaches her final 2 months of fieldwork, she is asked to reflect on her experiences in preparation for the end-of-term field evaluation. Natasia was eager to start her internship and chose to work in an urban agency that had a diverse client population. Having been raised in a family that believed that all people should be treated equally, and having lived most of her life in a small rural all-white community, Natasia was looking forward to the challenges of an urban experience.

Natasia's agency is located in an active urban community that is home to a growing LGB population. At this community agency, clients can find a diverse range of services all under one roof. The rapid growth of the community, however, has required changes within the agency, which is often short staffed. Although clients from various identity groups are served, the agency staff is primarily composed of white Western European, middle-class, heterosexual women. Natasia looks to her colleagues and supervisor to understand agency protocol in this rapidly changing environment.

Natasia has demonstrated her willingness to actively engage in reflective practice through the use of supervision, journal writing, and field seminar discussions. Her weekly meetings with her supervisor have been very task focused, and she has received positive feedback about her performance. While reviewing her cases thus far, however, Natasia and her supervisor noticed a pattern in some of her closed cases. Clients who identified as heterosexual had better outcomes than clients who identified as lesbian, gay, or bisexual. Natasia was concerned with this revelation. She is committed to her work and believes in treating all people equally.

Natasia reviewed her cases and asked herself Kondrat's questions. As she evaluated her daily behavior, how she related to and interpreted the behavior of others, her intentions, and the consequences of her actions, she came to realize that in spite of her commitment to "equal" treatment, she inadvertently disregarded the history, culture, and value differences that significantly influence the ways in which sexual orientation affects an individual's experience of the world.

have been marginalized. This process helps one examine how power and privilege are understood or misunderstood, and how assumptions make a difference in determining whether interactions are productive, hurtful, or destructive. Identity differences in ethnicity, race, socioeconomic status, ability, citizenship status, sexual orientation, gender, and sex influence the interactions between members of privileged groups and people who are from historically oppressed populations.

Critical reflectivity allows people to begin to understand how their experience of themselves is embedded in their interactions with others and how shared meanings are created (D'Cruz et al., 2015). The focus is on examining the ways things can be changed, not on what could or should have happened. Moving beyond guilt, shame, or anger to critical reflection facilitates growth and the development of a new social consciousness (Schmitz, Stakeman, & Sisneros, 2001). Misinformation that was received in the past can be corrected and behavior modified into the future.

Understanding oneself in context allows one to search for new explanations for our behavior and intentions (Schmitz et al., 2001). In this process, personal biases and cultural stereotypes, societal prejudices and oppression, and the experiences of ethnoracial groups in modern society are examined. It is within the context of experiences, relationships, family, community, and culture that we interpret daily interactions. Understanding ourselves involves examining the norms, values, and skills arising from our racial, ethnic, gender, socioeconomic, ability, citizenship, religion, and sexual orientation history and identification.

As we engage in the process, we may come to recognize the disparities in power and authority between ourselves and others, and begin to understand that our actions may have unintended consequences for others (Kondrat, 1999). Individuals who are white may recognize that they are members of a group that oppresses people from other ethnoracial groups, and that they are perceived as such by others. Collective knowledge of race relations and personal experience with racism may make people of color reticent to accept the actions of white individuals and groups. Similarly, white individuals and groups may feel the guilt and shame of racism, which can interfere with their interactions with others. Likewise, interactions between members of different populations of color are also influenced by assumptions, biases, and prejudices. Through dialogue, it is possible to build bridges across difference.

CONCLUSION

One of the often hidden phenomena of membership in a privileged group is the assumption of normality that defines "the other" as "not normal." Assumptions are too often built on mythology and belief in one's own normality. For instance, the assumption that growing up in a multiracial family or in a family with lesbian or gay parents can harm children is not based on data. People's interactions with others are influenced by myths like these. The consequences are destructive when working with children and families. With guidance, the experience of difference can lead to the development not only of a strong sense of self but also empathy, compassion, and understanding.

Racism, heterosexism and homophobia, sexism, transphobia, nationalism, and ableism are pervasive; even a person who sees herself or himself as unprejudiced can be guilty (Tatum, 1994). This realization can cause a broad range of emotions—including frustration, shame, fault, and guilt (Schmitz et al., 2001). These uncomfortable feelings should be acknowledged and examined to prevent creation of barriers to learning. Learning to recognize privileges that result from oppressive systems creates opportunities for transformative change. Examination of the learning process illuminates ways in which belief systems are shaped.

We enter this world without bias and prejudice toward others. However, through socialization, we are taught to value some identities and devalue others. Misinformation and stereotypes learned in the family are reinforced by the media, schools, religious institutions, government, and legal systems. Our self-identity can be bolstered or deflated depending on the social strata we occupy. The sense of ourselves as racist, sexist, classist, homophobic beings brings up a variety of emotions ranging from a false sense of superiority to a false sense of inferiority. At each stage of learning we consciously or unconsciously accept what we have been taught. These truths, as we come to know them, shape how we see ourselves and how we view others. As Nelson Mandela (1994) stated in *Long Walk to Freedom*,

> No one is born hating another person because of the color of his [or her] skin, or background, or religion. People must learn to hate, and if they can learn to hate, they can be taught to love, for love comes more naturally to the human heart than its opposite. (pp. xx)

Investigating one's self-identities and how they interfere with the ability to understand multiple worldviews can create opportunities for change. Start by examining your relationships and the patterns they follow. Becoming an agent for equality in a multicultural society requires one to accept this as a journey, not a destination. It also requires us to live with vulnerability as we navigate new paths and grow to understand, if not accept, other ways of knowing and being. In the end, we all want to be accepted both by people who are similar to us and by those who are not, and see the "end of what [are] very artificial and arbitrary division[s]" (Ackah, 1999, n.p.).

Questions for Consideration

1. Learning can begin with basic questions. Take time to explore your feelings as you answer these questions. Who is in your family and your social and community circles? With whom do you socialize? What activities do you attend, and who else attends? How do you behave and interact with people from different cultures and communities? What are your assumptions about people from identities different from yours? How can you create opportunities to form supportive and meaningful relationships with people from other cultures and communities?

2. White privilege is embedded into white supremacy; but most people with white privilege are not white supremacists. Reflect on how you see white privilege as different from white supremacy.

3. What are examples of white supremacy in your country? Change and knowledge building can be integrated into ongoing activities by expanding exposure to diverse peoples and experiences. Movies, books, museums, and activities can be labs for learning. Identify opportunities for learning, engage in those activities, and reflect on what you learned about yourself and others.

CHAPTER 3

Race, Ethnicity, Color, Caste, Tribe, and Nationality

Race is not biological. It is a social construct. There is no gene or cluster of genes common to all blacks or all whites.

>—Onwuachi-Willig, *According to Our Hearts*, 2013, p. 1

The very ink with which all history is written is merely fluid prejudice.

>—Mark Twain, *Following the Equator*, 1897

Race, ethnicity, color, caste, tribe, and nationality[1] are all social constructs that are used to identify and categorize people across the world. Globally, race is often seen as the master status that determines whether or not one is seen as superior to others. However, on the local level, race may or may not hold the most influence over how a person is treated. For example, one can easily argue that globally, people with lighter colored skin are privileged. Even within peoples of the same race, ethnicity, caste, tribe, and nationality, those with lighter skin are usually viewed by others more favorably than those with darker skin. The designation of color varies across the globe such that

> a person ascribed as black in the United States would likely not be considered black in Brazil, since each country has very different social institutions regarding the division of humanity into distinct races. (James, 2016, n.p.)

1. Each of these social identities can be further explored with additional readings. In this chapter, we introduce the topics and acknowledge that these social constructs are complex, nuanced, and vary across time and geopolitical realities. There are exceptions to every construction. For example, the designation of being "black" in South Africa could be tempered by those who were wealthy, despite the color of their skin.

Examining race, ethnicity, caste, color, tribe, and nationality in a specific location may reveal that race and color are not the most influential identities. For example, in the Arab Gulf, nationality and then tribe, followed by color, are of greater importance in determining where one falls in the hierarchy of privilege and oppression than race or ethnicity. Similarly, caste identity may "override other social identities, because of its primary importance for many South Asians" (Judge & Bal, 2008; as cited in Sankaran, Sekerdej, & von Hecker, 2017, n.p.)

Critical multiculturalism asks how social constructions of race, ethnicity, color, caste, tribe, and nationality are used and for whose benefit. Popular culture mediates images of what is believed to be the norm, which changes over time. These images often foster the belief that only certain groups have contributed to the development of society. What is glaringly absent is the recognition that each group makes rich and positive cultural contributions to a society.

As far back as 400 BCE, ancient Greeks classified people based on purely cultural differences like language, religion, and customs. Hierarchies in society were based on social standing rather than on appearance. The idea of classifying peoples based on their appearances did not come about until much later in history. In 1680 AD, the idea of classification by appearance slowly began to permeate society as lawmakers in the early colonies of North America began to use "white" as a classification of themselves rather than "Englishmen" or "Christians." In 1776 CE, the word *Caucasian* was first used by a man named Johann Blumenbach in his work *On the Natural Varieties of Mankind*. Blumenbach outlines one of the first hierarchies based on skin color, placing "whites" on top with four "races" underneath. The purpose of classification by race for people was to create a permanent class of slaves in the New World by homogenizing and identifying Europeans as white and creating other categories of people based on physical characteristics (Smedly, 2007). According to UNESCO (1950):

> many national, religious, geographic, linguistic, or cultural groups have, in such loose usage, been called races, when obviously Americans are not a race, nor are Englishmen, nor Frenchmen, nor any other national group. Catholics, Protestants, Moslems [sic], and Jews are not races, nor are groups who speak English or any other language thereby definable as a race, people who live in Iceland or England or India are not races; nor are people who are culturally Turkish or Chinese or the like thereby describable as races. (p. 2)

RACE, ETHNICITY, AND COLOR

Race is a social construction that is essentially the product of social thought and relations (Yudell, 2014). It is a concept that has different meaning to different people; the term itself can be inflammatory. Scientists have established that race is not linked to genetics (Yudell, 2014). Although people from different continents may have different skin color, eye shape, height, and hair type, these physical characteristics determine only a small part of who we are as humans. The social sciences have come to reject biological notions of race and now embrace the concept of race as a social construction (Onwuachi-Willig, 2016; Yudell, 2014).

The Social Construction of Race

Although there is debate about the origins of the idea of race, the first practice based on blood lineage appears to have occurred in the Iberian Peninsula at the turn of the 15th century when the Catholic monarchs Isabel and Ferdinand sought to create a purely Christian state by removing all Jews and Muslims. To ensure that only faithful Christians remained, they not only considered one's stated faith but also looked to ancestral lineage to ensure purity of blood (*limpieza de sangre*) (Hering Torres, 2012). Many believe this laid the way for later constructions of race based on physical characteristics. It is also suggested that this region may have been the origin of the idea of non-whites as inferior to whites (James, 2016). According to Fredrickson and Camarillo (2015), medieval Arabs and Moors had white and black slaves and although they did not base slavery purely on race, menial and degrading tasks were generally assigned to people who were black African. The use of black Africans, rather than whites, as slaves was further reinforced by the use of black Africans by light-skinned and tawny skinned slave owners of southern Iberia slaves. Christians and Muslims started to

> associate sub-Saharan African ancestry with lifetime servitude. When Portuguese navigators acquired slaves of their own as a result of their voyages along the Guinea Coast in the mid- to late fifteenth century and offered them for sale in the port cities of Christian Iberia, the identification of black skins with servile status was complete. (p. 29)

In 1684, Francois Bernier first used the concept of race when he identified "four or five species or races of men in particular whose difference is so remarkable that it may be properly made use of as the foundation for a new division of the earth" (Bernasconi & Lott, 2000, pp. 1–2). He saw differences in facial features, bone structure, hair, and skin color; he did, however, allow for some differences in skin color within a race.

Racism

Racism is structured around three flawed basic assumptions. First is the assumption that people can be divided into discrete categories based on biology. Second, these divisions are believed to be intrinsically connected to culture and individual characteristics such as personality and intelligence. Finally, it is assumed that due to "biological" race, some groups are naturally superior to others (Marger, 1997). The very ordinariness of racism is what makes it so difficult to change. It is the common way of doing business and benefits people who are white across classes (Delgado & Stefancic, 2017).

People's first inclination is to see racism as tied to overtly racist regimes under which the unequal treatment of people based on race is bureaucratized and rationalized. This can be seen in the apartheid of South Africa and the Western history of slavery. Racism is institutionalized (i.e., normalized) to the point that we tolerate it as part of everyday life. Racism can be subtle or blatant, overt or covert. It can be disguised in everyday interactions; and it can be found in the unintended—and intended—consequences of policy and practice.

Racism is not just a personal ideology but a system of cultural messages and institutional policies and practices, as well as individual beliefs and actions. Across the globe, this system clearly operates to the advantage of whites and to the disadvantage of people of color. Racial prejudice, when combined with social power and access to social, cultural, and economic resources and decision making, leads to the institutionalization of racist policies and practices. Racism is a structural issue, and only those with the political and economic power to oppress others can be racist (Bivens, 1995). Therefore, although people from any ethnoracial group can be prejudiced or biased and practice discrimination, only those with the resources to oppress other groups systemically and structurally can be correctly identified as racist (Rosaldo, 1993).

Some of the social and political manifestations of racism can be seen in laws, such as those forbidding interracial marriage; designating separate facilities for blacks and whites, including public transportation, schools, and bathrooms; ordering the internment of Japanese Americans in the United States during World War II; and enforcing higher penalties for crack cocaine than powder cocaine. In South Africa, under apartheid, access to goods and services for all non-white people was systematically controlled. The strictest limitations were applied to people with the darkest skin color (Patterson, 1953). Nazi Germany engaged in mass genocide in an attempt to create a perfect society made up of a "perfect" white, blond, blue-eyed race. Racism can be seen in policies and practices that structure barriers to keep people of color from gaining equal access to resources such as quality education, decent housing, and economic opportunities that could enable people of color to move out of poverty.

Color and the Privileging of Whiteness

Color is another construct that can be used to create social identities. Although color is often seen as interchangeable with race or ethnicity, color crosses divisions between and within various ethnoracial groups. Because people who are white (privileged) do not generally perceive themselves in racial terms, discussions about race usually refer to people who are marginalized; often black/African, Latino/Latina, Asian, and/or indigenous/aboriginal people but rarely to those in privileged groups (i.e., people viewed as white). When forced to acknowledge their whiteness/privilege, they see it as not being black, or not being the "other." This allows them to avoid acknowledging the centrality of ethnoracial identity in both daily interactions and systemic economic and political structures.

Because race is a social construction based on hierarchical divisions of power and privilege, the concept of whiteness has been invisible. Lopez (1996) calls this the "transparency phenomenon," whereby people's whiteness renders them invisible or transparent. As a result of this phenomenon, people who are white have the privilege of not being conscious of their own racial identity and are not required to understand the implications of being white. The invisibility of whiteness privileges leads many people who are viewed as white to believe they are "normal," the standard by which all others are judged. Wildman and Davis (2002) write that

> the invisibility of privilege strengthens and maintains the power it creates. The invisible cannot be combated, and as a result privilege is allowed to perpetuate, regenerate, and re-create itself. Privilege is systemic, not an occasional occurrence. Privilege is invisible only until looked for, but silence in the face of privilege sustains invisibility. (p. 89)

Although currently whiteness is seen globally as the norm, the standard for being, this was not always the case. It was not until the end of the seventeenth century that an interest in white identity developed. The institutionalization of the system of race privilege through slavery made it necessary to make clear distinctions between blacks and whites (Allen, 2012). In the United States, a legal definition of whiteness was not established until immigration laws were drafted in 1790 and the courts began making decisions concerning who could and could not live in the United States and what rights those living in the United States would have. Judges defined whiteness based on prejudices of the time as the absence of blackness, an opposition that marked a boundary between those with privilege and those without. Only those deemed white were worthy of entry into the United States under early immigration statutes (Lopez, 1996).

In South Africa, whiteness was also privileged. The Dutch colonizers arriving in the late 1700s passed legislation separating white colonists from native blacks. This segregation continued after South African independence from Britain, with the 1913 Land Act that moved people identified as black to special reserves, leaving the majority of the land to the white minority. Apartheid (which literally means "separation") was strengthened following World War II with the Population Registration Act of 1950 that classified all people into race: white, colored (mixed race), black (Bantu), and Asian (Act No, 30 of 1950). Marriage and sexual intercourse were banned between whites and people of other races, facilities were segregated (schools, beaches, post offices, etc.), and only people identified as white could participate in the national government. In segregated South Africa, whites were at the top of the social ladder, Asians and colored had less power than whites but more than blacks, and blacks were at the bottom of the hierarchy (Posel, 2001). It is important to note, however, that "official categories of race were . . . defined and enacted in ways which connected them closely to factors of lifestyle and social standing" as much as the actual color of one's skin (Posel, 2001, p. 89).

In Australia, the invasion by European colonists brought with them the derogatory use of the term "black." Arriving in Australia in 1770, Lt. James Cook claimed Australia for the British crown, declaring the island "terras nullus" (meaning no one's land) despite the fact that over 400 nations inhabited the land prior to Cook's claim. Using the term "black" with the same negative connotations used in the Americas, the colonists identified Aborigines as subhuman, as noted in this journal entry by Bishop Polding (1845):

> I have myself heard a man, educated, and a large proprietor of sheep and cattle, maintain that there was no more harm in shooting a native, than in shooting a wild dog. I have heard it maintained by others that it is the course of

Providence, that blacks should disappear before the white, and the sooner the process was carried out the better, for all parties. I fear such opinions prevail to a great extent. Very recently in the presence of two clergymen, a man of education narrated, as a good thing, that he had been one of a party who had pursued the blacks, in consequence of cattle being rushed by them, and that he was sure that they shot upwards of a hundred. When expostulated with, he maintained that there was nothing wrong in it, that it was preposterous to suppose they had souls. (Aboriginal Heritage Office, 2017, n.p.)

Early references to Aborigines used the term "black or Aboriginal natives" to refer to the original inhabitants of Australia (see, for example, the proclamation by His Excellency Colonel George Arthur, Lieutenant Governor of the Island of Van Diemen's Land and its Dependencie, 1828).[2] Many of the policies adopted by the colonists with reference to Aborigines, for example segregation and forced removal,

were driven by assumptions about the possibility of "breeding out" the Aboriginal race. At the heart of such sentiment lies a vision of Aboriginal identity that relies primarily on skin colour, or "racial (im)purity," rather than familial and cultural ties and acceptance by members of an Aboriginal community. (Bird, 2011, n.p.)

Brazil is another excellent country to examine when considering the importance of color over race or ethnicity. After slavery was abolished in 1890, the Brazilian census did not ask about race, but instead asked respondents to identify their color (white, black, yellow, red, or brown). At the same time, certain traits were attributed to people based on the color of their skin, with valued traits connected to people who were viewed as white (for example, rationality) and traits that were not seen as valuable attributed to people with darker skin (for example, creativity) (Nolen, 2015).

Ethnicity and Ethnoracial Identity

Ethnicity, like race, is socially constructed. An ethnic group is usually defined as being composed of people who share a sense of attachment on the basis of cultural criteria and a shared history. It can be tempting to use ethnicity instead of race as an identifier because it appears to move away from

2. Available at http://trove.nla.gov.au/newspaper/article/4219798

the notion that this source of identity is biological or natural (Smedley, 2007). What is important to understand is how populations self-identity across cultural, affiliative, and subjective dimensions. Ethnicity is fluid, flexible, layered, and dependent on circumstances and context.

Current scholars of race and ethnic relations have adopted the concept of ethnoracial identity to more accurately describe the complexity of people's experiences and to acknowledge how the concepts of race and ethnicity have collided. The theoretical construct of ethnoracial identity forces us to remember that history, people's physical attributes, and culture define the course of people's lives. Ethnoracial identity acknowledges that people respond to both physical and cultural cues in others. Ethnoracial groups are neither simple nor static categories. They are created among the social relationships through which people distinguish themselves from others (Wimmer, 2008).

The categories of race and ethnicity can be limiting when they are used in practice, rather than theory, to identify people in need of services rather than as abstract concepts. Ethnoracial positioning can provide a more accurate understanding of an individual, family, or community. In exploring ethnoracial identity, one can move beyond categories such as black or white to look at the values, beliefs, attitudes, activities, behaviors, and practices that affect people's daily lives and community identification. The exploration of ethnoracial positioning might require learning about nationality; the language the family speaks at home; and different aspects of the culture, including child-rearing practices, milestone celebrations, kin relationships, and gender role expectations. Illness and health, as well as the role of authority, are viewed in different ways depending on the family's ethnoracial identification. Depending on their ethnoracial identification, the family could experience support or marginalization within their larger community. Although still not perfect, these factors allow for a deeper understanding than the concept of race alone.

Mixed Ethnoracial Identity

Despite the efforts of some groups to maintain ethnoracial "purity,"[3] the number of people who identify as being of mixed ethnic or racial[4] heritage

3. Racial purity is another social construction.
4. "Persons who are multiethnic may not identify as multiracial. For example, a person who identifies monoracially as white may identify multiethnically because her ethnic heritage includes Italian, Irish, and Norwegian" (Samuels, 2014, p. 5).

is increasing across the globe. People with mixed race or ethnic identities arise primarily from a history of colonization, occupation, migration, and conquest, although recent increases in global media and communication, travel, tourism, and humanitarian work have also contributed to mixed race/ethnic identities (King-O'Riain & Small, 2014). Many countries have attempted to curb mixed race or ethnic relationships through laws against interracial marriage (United States, South Africa), denying citizenship to mixed race children (Japan, Britain), and segregation of people identified as belonging to distinct racial or ethnic groups (United States, South Africa).

Social attitudes toward people who identify as mixed race or mixed ethnicity are changing, and probably affect the increasing number of people who are comfortable identifying as being of mixed racial or ethnic heritage (King-O'Riain & Small, 2014). That is not to say that persons of mixed race or ethnicity no longer experience stigma, discrimination, and/or oppression. In fact, people with mixed race or ethnic identity may experience discrimination based on any of their racial or ethnic identities, in addition to being discriminated against because they are mixed (Nadal et al., 2010; Samuels, 2009).

The social constructions of race and identity are not based on genetic or biological factors, but rather are ways of organizing status and meaning in the world. Therefore, ideas of race and ethnicity change over time. In the past, the United States considered persons of mixed black and white heritage to be black, if they had even "one drop of black blood." However, since 2000, the United States has allowed respondents to identify as more than one race when completing the census.

CASTE, TRIBE, AND NATIONALITY

Caste, tribe, and nationality are social constructs that are often used to privilege one group while disadvantaging others. In the same way that humans created the categories of race and ethnicity, humans created the categories of caste, tribe, and nationality. All three are identities assigned at birth, usually based upon the status of a child's parents, and are generally unchanged throughout one's life. Even nationality often remains the same even if one immigrates and becomes a citizen of another country.

Caste

Caste systems are defined as "ranked, hereditary, endogamous occupational groups that constitute traditional societies in certain regions of the world" ("Caste system," 2017). The hierarchies created in the Hindu caste system are based on the social constructs of "purity" and "pollution" (Singh, 2008) and "filth" and "cleanliness" (Human Rights Watch, 2001b). In South Asia, the caste system divides people into different social categories, with Brahmins considered the highest caste (priests and teachers), followed by Kshatriyas (rulers and soldiers), Vaisyas (merchants and traders), and Sudras (laborers and artisans) (Rao, 2010). Dalits (untouchables) are outside of the caste system (Rao, 2010). Researchers have stressed the importance of caste as a social identity in South Asia when compared to other social identities like gender and ethnicity (see, for example, Gayer, 2000; Mand, 2006). It is important to note that "lower-caste communities are almost invariably indistinguishable in physical appearance from higher caste communities. This is not, as some would say, a black and white issue" (Human Rights Watch, 2001b, p. 2).

Although India is often the first country we think of when we hear the word *caste*, caste systems have existed for over 2,000 years and have occurred in most countries around the world. Despite local and international bans on caste, they continue to exist to some degree in many countries, including but not limited to Mauritania, Nigeria, Senegal, South Africa, Bangladesh, Japan, Korea, Nepal, Pakistan, and Sri Lanka (Human Rights Watch, 2001b).

It is currently estimated that over 260,000,000 people face discrimination based on caste (International Dalit Solidarity Network, n.d.). This includes the "Dalits, untouchables of South Asia—including Nepal, Bangladesh, India, Sri Lanka, and Pakistan—as well as the Buraku people of Japan, the Osu of Nigeria, and certain groups in Senegal and Mauritania who also suffer from caste-based discrimination" (Human Rights Watch, 2001b, p. 1). This discrimination includes segregation in education, employment, housing, and health care. The impact of discrimination is poverty, debt bondage, and slavery for many of those in the "untouchable" castes around the world. At the intersection of gender and class, low-caste women are particularly vulnerable to sexual assault, violence, and trafficking.

Tribe

Tribe is another word used to describe social groupings based on "social, economic, religious, or blood ties" ("Tribe," 2017). Although the origin of the word *tribe* is debated, it is the term that was used to describe the division of the Roman state (circa 240 BCE) into three ethnic groups and in the Bible to describe the 12 lineages of Hebrews who settled in the

Promised Land (Lowe, 2001). Translations of the Latin word *tribe* into Greek and Hebrew suggest that the word was used interchangeably with "race" or "clan."

Although historically the use of the word *tribe* was acceptable, in the current context it is often associated with the negative attitudes of white colonists toward people they saw as savages, primitive, and uncivilized (Lowe, 2001). The labeling of people as tribesmen—and therefore as "less than"—supported slavery and white colonial rule in the Americas, Africa, and Australia (Pauls, 2008). For example, white colonists saw all Africans as living in tribes, ignoring the fact that

> their ancestors built large trading empires and Muslim universities on the Niger River, densely settled and cultivated kingdoms around the great lakes in east-central Africa, or lived in much smaller-scale communities between the larger political units of the continent. Calling nearly all African social groups "tribes" and African identities "tribal" in the era of scientific racism turned the idea of tribe from a social science category into a racial stereotype. (Africa Policy Information Center, 1997, p. 5)

In South Africa, the use of the words *tribe* and *tribal* blurred the true nature of the deadly conflict between followers of the African National Congress and the Inkatha Freedom Party (Africa Policy Information Center, 1997). This conflict is often portrayed as reflecting "primitivism and ancient tribal rivalries," which is misleading (Africa Policy Information Center, p. 6).

> Under South African rule, the term "tribe" referred to an administrative unit governed by a chief under rules imposed by the white government. Tribes were thus not ancient and traditional, but modern bureaucratic versions of the old small kingdoms. . . . In the early 1990s the violence spread to the Johannesburg area and often took the ethnic form of Zulu IFP followers vs. Xhosa ANC followers. Yet this was not an ancient tribal conflict either, since historically the independent Zulu and Xhosa nations never fought a war. Rather it was a modern, urban, politicized ethnic conflict. (Africa Policy Information Center, p. 6)

Colonial administrators in North America often incorrectly grouped diverse indigenous groups together as a single tribe. For example, the name "Sioux" (meaning Snake) was applied incorrectly to a group of people they thought were unified, even though the people they called Souix were diverse linguistically and politically (Pauls, 2008). By the 19th century, white colonists decided that people who spoke Dakota, Lakota, and Nakota were bands within the greater Sioux nation, even though these three groups represent different linguistic, and not just political, divisions (Pauls, 2008).

Nationality

Nationality and *citizenship* are often used interchangeably, but they are not the same terms. Nationality refers to the country or region where one is born and is often closely related to ethnicity. Citizenship, on the other hand, is a legal relationship a person has with a country, which usually includes the right to hold a passport and vote. Someone can be a national and not be a citizen, and vice versa. For example, in the United States, a person born in American Samoa or Swains Island is a US national, but not a citizen. On the other hand, a person born in the territories of Guam, Puerto Rico, or the US Virgin Islands is considered a citizen of the United States and can vote and hold political office. In Mexico, a person is considered a national upon birth, but not awarded citizenship until they are 18 years old.

As noted earlier, the word *nationality* is often used interchangeably with *ethnicity*, resulting in some countries recognizing multiple nationalities within their borders. In the former Soviet Union, "nationality" was understood as "ethnicity" and the Union of Soviet Socialist Republics (USSR) formally recognized over 100 ethnic groups as nationalities. As of 1978, Spain recognizes 17 autonomous communities as nationalities, including Galicians, Basques, and Catalans. People in each of the 17 regions have a strong sense of their historical and cultural identity (Muro & Guiroga, 2005). Citizens of the Jewish state of Israel can identify as "Jewish nationality," "Arab nationality," or "Druze nationality" (Columbia Law School, 2017).

There are also people who have a strong sense of national identity but who have no internationally recognized state for their nationality. For example, Kurds usually identify their nationality as Kurdish, even though Kurdistan is currently not an internationally recognized state. When Israel was created in 1948, the majority of Arab-Palestinians became stateless, but they did not lose their sense of national identity as Palestinians (Columbia Law School, 2017). Interestingly, the Israeli Supreme Court determined that there was no "Israeli nationality" because a person could not have two nationalities—in this case, Israeli and Jewish nationalities (Columbia Law School, 2017).

Example

In 2010, during video conference exchanges between students from the Arab Gulf and students in the United States, participants from the Arab Gulf introduced themselves by nationality (Qatari, Yemeni, Saudi, etc.). When US students of color introduced themselves, they identified themselves by ethnicity (African American, Mexican, Salvadoran, Asian American, etc.). But when white students introduced themselves, they made no reference to nationality, race, ethnicity, or heritage.

MIGRATION AND IMMIGRATION

All nonindigenous people have migrated.[5] Beginning with the movement out of Africa 70,000 years ago, people migrated across Australia, Asia, and Europe by 40,000 years BCE, followed by migration to the Americas 20,000–15,000 years ago with more recent migrations such as the Neolithic Revolution, Indo-European expansion, and the Early Medieval Great Migrations (Zerjal, Spencer Wells, Yuldasheva, Ruzibakiev, & Tyler-Smith, 2002). Migration continues to change the population of sending and receiving countries around the globe, with over 244 million people migrating internationally in 2015 (United Nations Department of Economic and Social Affairs, 2016). Between 2000 and 2015, migration contributed to 42% of the population growth in North America and 32% in Oceania (United Nations Department of Economic and Social Affairs). During the same time period, Europe would have fallen in population if it weren't for migration (United Nations Department of Economic and Social Affairs). On the other hand, population growth slowed in Africa, Asia, Latin America, and the Caribbean, due to negative net migration (United Nations Department of Economic and Social Affairs).

There are many countries where migrants are the majority of the population, including China, Macao Special Administrative Region (58%); Bahrain (51%); Kuwait (74%); Qatar (75%); United Arab Emirates (88%); Channel Islands (50%); Isle of Man (52%); Andorra (60%); Liechtenstein (63%); Monaco (56%); Bonaire, Saint Eustatius, and Saba (52%); British Virgin Islands (57%); Saint Maarten (Dutch part) (70%); US Virgin Islands (53%); Falkland Islands (Malvinas) (54%); and Venezuela (50%) (United Nations,

---

5. *Migration* refers to movement, usually temporary, from one place to another. *Immigration* means to come to a country for the purpose of living there permanently. *Emigration* means to go to another country.

2016). Most immigrants to these countries are workers legally admitted to fill gaps in the local workforce. Therefore, the immigrant's right to be in the country is based upon employment, which may result in deportation once employment is ended, even for those who may have lived in the country most, or—in the case of workers' children—all of their lives. The threat of deportation prevents many immigrants from complaining about poor work conditions, exploitation, and abuse.

As international migration continues to grow, so does discrimination and exploitation against newcomers. Although anti-immigrant sentiments can limit job opportunities for migrants, some employers seek out migrants because they can be more easily exploited. Around the globe, immigrants often experience discrimination in employment (hiring, promotions, pay); housing; health care; education; and social welfare (United Nations, 2017). Recent immigrants to Europe and North America are exposed to racist remarks by political leaders, police violence, and anti-immigrant protests. This can add to already existing negative impacts due to the trauma of war, poor health resulting from poverty in the home country, and the loss of family and community due to migration. Discrimination against immigrants is closely tied to racism and xenophobia, and intersects with gender, socioeconomic status, and religion (Soylu & Buchanon, 2013).

CONCLUSION

For centuries, humans have placed people into categories based on religion, language, and customs. However, the concept of race—categorizing people based on physical appearance such as color of skin or facial features in a way that valued certain groups over others—was a phenomenon of Western colonizers justifying the use of Africans as slaves. Ethnicity, color, caste, tribe, and nationality are also social constructs used to categorize people, with certain people in each identity category privileged while others are marginalized and oppressed. These systems of oppression have led to economic inequality, health disparities, and even statelessness for millions of people around the globe.

Examination of the multiple categories people occupy (or are delegated to), including race/ethnicity, caste, tribe, gender/sex, nationality, sexual orientation, and ability/disability, reveals the complexity of the multiple mechanisms of oppression. These identity categories, and others, constitute separate forms of marginalization. Further, individuals who occupy more than one of these categories experience an additional marginalization at the intersection of oppressions (Delgado & Stefancic, 2017).

Individuals and communities of color experience Young's five faces of oppression. People of color face economic exploitation and marginalization due to structural barriers embedded into the political, social, and economic systems. Without understanding that various statuses and structures intersect to create what Frye (2000) refers to as a cage, we cannot see the constraints that hold people in place, preventing them from exercising their full potential. When race, ethnicity, color, caste, color, and nationality are used to determine who has access to goods and services; when gender/sex, ability, and/or sexual orientation are used to determine worthiness; and when parental access to privilege determines access to quality education, we rob people of the right to determine their own fate. They experience the oppression of overlapping systems that work to keep them powerless, amid the cultural imperialism that frames them as "the other."

Questions for Consideration

In your country,

1. What are the major racial, ethnic, color, caste, tribal, and/or nationality groups?
2. Which groups are privileged and which are oppressed based on race, ethnicity, color, caste, tribe, and/or nationality?
3. Which identity—race, ethnicity, color, caste, tribe, and/or nationality— is the master status in your country/region?
4. Has privilege and oppression of groups based on race, ethnicity, color, caste, tribe, and/or nationality changed over time and in what ways?
5. What are the economic impacts on people oppressed based on race, ethnicity, color, caste, tribe, and/or nationality?
6. What laws, policies, and/or regulations support the categorization, privileging, and oppression of people based on race, ethnicity, color, caste, tribe, and/or nationality?

CHAPTER 4

Gender, Sex, and Sexual Orientation

The emotional, sexual, and psychological stereotyping of females begins when the doctor says: "It's a girl."

> —Shirley Chisholm (as cited in Hoard, *Anthology: Quotations and Sayings of People of Color*, 1973)

We should all be feminists.

> —Chimamanda Ngozi Adichie, *We Should All Be Feminists*, 2014

Most of us have been taught that sex and gender are synonymous and that there are only two options: female or male. One of these two is usually assigned at birth. Socialization occurs based on that assignment. Based on the sex assigned, we grow up socialized to the designated gender role, which is socially constructed and culturally based (Lips, 2017). We come to understand that male is better than female and that we are all supposed to be heterosexual. This is assumed to be natural; these beliefs are implicit in our norms. The link between sex (biology) and gender (socially and culturally based roles) has long been taken for granted (Greene, 2000). Failure to follow gender role expectations, including those dictating the gender of those with whom we engage in sexual and romantic relationships, is considered unnatural and labeled as deviant. Understanding gender identity and sexual orientation requires us to understand the multifaceted experience of sex and gender. More recently, the connection has been recognized for its complexity (Baca Zinn, Hondagneu-Sotelo, Messner, & Denissen, 2016).

The privileging of males is evidenced in gender-based inequality, which is an issue across the globe (Lindsey, 2016). Although the United Nations

Development Program has worked to decrease the gender gap, gender inequality has increased (United Nations, 2013). Although overall human development is improving, gender disparity is an ongoing problem (Lindsey, 2016). Women are more likely to live in abject poverty, perform significant unpaid labor, be underrepresented in political systems, and be faced with a major employment inequality (Lindsey, 2016). Women face the highest levels of restrictions (see United Nations, 2013, for further study).

This discrimination against women is widespread, and the violation of the rights of women occurs on many levels on a daily basis. The media assists in promoting and maintaining disadvantages faced by women through ignoring, trivializing, judging, and distorting information about them. Images that prescribe what women should do, be like, or look like are powerful yet subtle vehicles of control. These images play a significant role in defining gender roles through everyday practices and discourses. They result in profound negative effects on all populations.

GENDER AND SEX

At birth, based on external genitalia, individuals are usually classified as male or female. This assignment starts a socialization process anchored in identity communities, social and political structures, and family dynamics. Although the terms *sex* and *gender* are too often used interchangeably, there is a clear difference between the two. *Sex* is a term that refers to the biology of genitalia and reproductive organs. Once sex is assigned at birth, a whole set of gender expectations is mapped onto this primary sex distinction (Bryson, 1999; Lindsey, 2016). *Gender*, however, is more than physical biology, and it is not a dichotomous phenomenon that defines an individual as either masculine or feminine (Baca Zinn et al., 2016; Fausto-Sterling, 1992; Garnets, 2002, Lindsey, 2016). Gender is a social construction that is shaped by social and cultural contexts and related to the roles, behaviors, and attitudes we expect from people based on their categorization as female or male. Gender roles are learned and interact with social structures (Baca Zinn et al., 2016; Bryson, 1999; Butler, 1999/2004). These social structures reinforce the inequality of women, and this is supported by patriarchal systems of male dominance. Sexual orientation, relational and sexual attraction, intersects with gender and sex and multiple additional identities, including race/ethnicity, religion, and nationality. It is used as a weapon of sexism at the interpersonal, structural, and cultural levels.

Cisgender, Transgender, and Intersex

The sex/gender lens is complex. Even though the myth is that all people are either male or female, in actuality, this is not the case. Once presumed to be a dichotomous choice, masculine or feminine is now understood as a gender continuum rather than a dichotomy. An individual's internal sense of gender is their "gender identity." A person may identify as female, male, intersex, transgender, or gender fluid. "Cisgender" is a label that refers to a person who identifies with the gender assigned at birth based on anatomy. They may identify as cis female, cis male, cis woman, or cis man. Someone who is gender fluid, on the other hand, does not identify with just one gender. Their gender identity may change across time; or they may identify as both male and female, or perhaps neither.

The term "intersex" refers to a diverse group of individuals who are born with genetic and chromosomal anomalies, and people with so-called ambiguous genitalia. For example, there are individuals born with an XX-XY chromosomal configuration, which means they have both male and female reproductive organs. Some are born with genitalia that appear to be somewhere between male and female. Too often surgery is performed on intersex infants before medical tests that identify sex can be conducted and the implications for the child as they mature can be considered. Parents of intersex children are frequently isolated and ill informed, having no medical or community support. Based on lack of knowledge, confusion, and fear, parents may follow the advice of professionals, who may also lack knowledge. Box 4.1 tells the story of an intersex individual.

The term *transgender*, on the other hand, refers to someone who does not self-identify with their sexual anatomy; it does not match the internal sense of their own sex and gender. Someone who is transgender may identify as female (trans woman) or male (trans man), or they may not identify as exclusively male or female. They may identify as gender-queer, bi-gender, pan-gender, gender-fluid, or a-gender. Current brain research suggests a possible biological basis underlying transgender identity (Russo, 2016).

With advances that have taken place in medical science since the early 1950s, it is possible for transgender individuals to go through hormonal treatments and have their anatomy altered through sexual reassignment surgery, sometimes called gender reassignment surgery. Only a small minority of people whose genitalia are inconsistent with their internal sense of their sex, however, seek sexual reassignment surgery (Wren, 2000). According to the Human Rights Campaign, only a third of transgender people undergo surgery (Molloy, 2014). Although it is hard to acquire global statistics, there are estimates that 25,000 gender reassignment surgeries

---

Box 4.1

I AM BOTH FEMALE AND MALE

I grew up a boy, socialized to a man's profession. As an engineer, I am successful in a "man's world." I design and contract out large projects. I married a woman as quiet as I am talkative. By the time I was 22 years of age, I had a son. I loved my wife deeply and we both believed in lifetime commitments.

Imagine my (our) surprise when I became ill, a life-threatening illness that baffled many experts. The diagnosis? Puberty—that is, my second puberty . . . puberty as a woman. This is what almost killed me. Unbeknownst to me or the doctors, I was menstruating internally and ended up with a terrible infection. While I was hospitalized for the infection, they discovered I had a uterus. I couldn't believe it. The feelings were overwhelming: fear, disbelief, grief, confusion.

Although the hospital social worker in our small city did not know much about intersex people or issues, she was compassionate and open. She took the time to explore the biological and social issues and found support and educational resources for my wife and me. The social worker provided information for the health professionals while also helping me and my wife through the crisis. I decided not to remove my uterus; instead, I managed the two sexes with hormones. In time, we had a second child, and I am now in menopause.

Over the years I have done a lot of reading and personal reflection. Because of my family and my career, I have chosen to live in the world as a man, and the world around me considers me a man. What I have come to recognize, however, is that internally, I identify as a woman—a woman in love with a woman. So, in many ways, my true identity remains hidden from those I love.

Only my wife knows, and she considers herself to be married to a man. There was some sadness in my decision not to tell others, but we worried about the impact that would have on our children. Now that I am retired, I am beginning to share my identity and life experience with others.

---

are performed annually (Scutti, 2014). It is important to realize that cisgender, transgender, and intersex people may identify as gay, straight, bisexual, or pansexual, and gender reassignment surgery may or may not be accompanied by a change in an individual's sexual orientation identity.

SEXUAL ORIENTATION

Sexual orientation refers to whether the preferred gender of one's romantic and/or sexual partner is the same, or different, from one's own gender. People who seek romantic and sexual partners who are the same gender as themselves are considered homosexual, lesbian, or gay. People who seek romantic and sexual partners who differ in gender from themselves are considered heterosexual. People who seek romantic and sexual partners who are either the same or other gender from themselves are considered bisexual (two), pansexual (all), polysexual (many), ambisexual (both), and/or omnisexual (all). Sexual orientation is thought of as existing on a continuum from heterosexual to homosexual, although one's identity may change over time and/or remain fluid.

Although the term *homosexual* did not exist until 1869, lesbian, gay, and bisexual (LGB) people have existed across time and cultures (Tully, 2000). In some contexts, LGB sexual orientations have been condemned; in others, they have been normalized and sometimes even exalted (Tully, 2000). Many indigenous cultures view sexuality and gender beyond the limits imposed by dominate cultures. Globally, there is rapid change regarding lesbian, gay, and bisexual, and transgender (LGBT) issues. However, the movement toward increasing legal and civil rights is accompanied by backlash from groups and individuals who feel disempowered by sharing privilege.

Increasing social and political awareness of LGB people and their issues has given rise to demands for recognition, acceptance, and rights in many countries. In 2011, the United Nations Human Rights Council passed its first resolution recognizing gay rights. LGBT rights movements range from social to political. Some have engaged activism and progressive movements. Reactions have ranged from progressive to violent and reactionary. Although lesbian and gay people have always formed partnerships, joined families, and raised children, they are now more visible in many societies than they have been historically. This has precipitated new demands for legal recognition of their relationships and families. In some countries, greater awareness has increased the danger for people who are lesbian and gay.

The move to legitimize gay marriage has made headway in many countries. As of July 2017, marriage for same-sex couples is legal in 24 countries, including Argentina, Belgium, Brazil, Canada, Colombia, Denmark, Finland, France, Germany, Iceland, Ireland, Luxembourg, Malta, Mexico, the Netherlands, New Zealand, Norway, Portugal, South Africa, Spain, Sweden, the United Kingdom, the United States, and Uruguay. On the African continent, only South Africa recognizes gay marriage. Recognition of same-sex marriage has legal, economic, political, and social implications. The push to gain rights continues with efforts to pass nondiscrimination laws in employment, housing, and adoption; bans on conversion therapy; and hate crimes legislation.

Unfortunately, the backlash in response to this change has gained momentum as well. Recently, some countries have expanded anti-LGB laws. For example, although Uganda has had antigay laws since colonialism, in 2013 the possible punishment for engaging in same-sex sexual behavior was increased to life in prison. Four countries still enforce the death penalty for same-sex sexual behavior: Yemen, Kingdom of Saudi Arabia, Iran, and Sudan (ILGA, 2017). Russia decriminalized same-sex sexual activity in 1993 but recently enacted a law banning promotion of same-sex sexual behavior among minors (ILGA, 2017). And several countries have recently criminalized same-sex sexual activity between women, when previously only same-sex sexual activity between men was illegal (e.g., Solomon Islands, Botswana).

THE ENFORCEMENT OF GENDER ROLES

Gender socialization begins when the sex/gender of the child is known. It is the strongest indicator of how family interact with the child; and it is a major determinant of toys, games, and colors directed at the child (Lindsey, 2016; Szegedy-Maszak, 2001). Latency age peer groups further the gender socialization process as major contributors to the development of homophobia (Birkett & Espelage, 2015). They often influence and support a name-calling process that sets the stage for increasing the risk for structural and physical violence, self-inflicted injury, depression, and isolation of those targeted. A boy who is not willing to engage in the aggressive games and behaviors that are usually expected of boys may be referred to as a "pink boy" or, in the United States, as a "sissy," an abbreviation for sister. These labels suggest inferiority of the boy in question and all females; similar themes are often used to demean people who are lesbian or gay, linking sexual orientation with gendered oppression. "One of the social functions of the persecution of 'the sissy' is to force other boys into gender role compliance" (Brooks, 2000, p. 108). Boys, as well as girls, who do not comply, face isolation and persecution.

Gender roles, the belief that certain roles are appropriate only for women or only for men, are socially constructed (Burr, 1995; Lindsey, 2016; Lips, 2017). They are not just biological; rather, they are social and psychological constructs (Somech & Drach-Zahavy, 2016). The assignment of the labels "masculine" and "feminine" to every aspect of human behavior often results in rigid expectations that affect both females and males. Gender role expectations impact individuals' occupational choice; type of behavior as a worker, spouse, or parent; and work–family relations (Lindsey, 2016;

Somech & Drach-Zahavy, 2016, p, 1). The intersections of race, ethnicity, nationality, class, and caste shape gender roles; however, masculinity is universally privileged over femininity (Baca Zinn et al., 2016; Lindsey, 2016; Lips, 2017).

There are consequences for individuals who exhibit gender-noncon-forming behavior, that is, behavior that falls outside the bounds of what has been identified as masculine or feminine based on social assumptions and traditions. Those who violate the rules and regulations that govern gender roles by not conforming are often ostracized, marginalized, stigmatized, and mistreated. Feminist literature and studies on boys emphasize the harmful effects that the enforcement of rigid gender roles has on children. Families, peers, schools, and social systems participate in the processes of gender socialization, nudging children and youth toward desired behavior (Lindsey, 2016). In preschool, the stereotypical gender roles started in the family are institutionalized as "appropriate" behavior (Lindsey, 2016). For example, if a boy tries to play at cooking with the girls, often at least one of the girls is likely to turn him away, chastising him for trying to play a girl's game (Szegedy-Maszak, 2001). Research has indicated that the play behavior of preschool boys is also regulated by other boys (Lippa, 2005). The more children segregate by gender, the less interested they are in breaking gender stereotypes (Lippa, 2005; Szegedy-Maszak, 2001).

Patriarchy interacts with gender socialization, pushing boys toward masculinity. At the far end of the continuum is toxic masculinity, when masculinity is defined as unemotional, aggressive, and rejecting. Toxic or hypermasculinity is posited as one of the underlying causes of violence, inequity, oppression, and conflict in human relationships, including war and interpersonal violence (Karp, 2010). Pollack and Shuster (2000), who have studied boys, note the "gender straightjacket" (p. 9) and lament that "society is pushing them to be just one kind of person, nudging them at a very young age to disconnect from their loved ones and to sacrifice that part within themselves that is genuinely loving, caring, and affectionate" (p. 5). Studies show that older boys are strongly impacted by this peer pressure (Lippa, 2005).

There are differences in gender role expectations based on nationality and culture. In Poland, Canada, and the United States, males are more likely to score higher on assertiveness than females; this is not the case in Finland and China (Lips, 2017). In the United States, males of all ethnic groups scored above the mean on self-esteem; black females were the only females who scored above the mean. Starting in adolescence, girls drop in self-esteem and assertiveness, whereas boys overtake girls in self-esteem and assertiveness. Adolescent girls score higher in anxiety and depression;

boys are more likely to be narcissistic and see themselves as smarter and more attractive (Lips, 2017). Pipher (1994) described a culture that splits adolescent girls into "true and false selves. The culture is what causes girls to abandon their true selves and take up false selves" (p. 37). She calls our culture "girl-poisoning" (p. 28). It is frightening to realize how toxic culture can be for both boys and girls who feel that they must amputate parts of their emotional selves to survive in their social environments.

Both boys and girls may benefit from greater freedom in gender roles (Lindsey, 2016). Studies show the value of gender role flexibility; role flexibility is less constraining and creates a path to an increase in gender equality (Lindsey, 2016). Individuals, based on context and strengths, can engage flexibility traits. Studies indicate that a level of androgyny creates a healthier life. Androgyny does not mean that everyone is the same; rather, it refers to the ability to nurture traits in the self wherever they fall on the socially constructed female/male continuum. Androgyny involves the integration of traits considered feminine and masculine (Lindsey, 2016). According to Cook (1985), "It is widely believed today that strict adherence to sex-appropriate standards for characteristics and behavior can adversely affect the psychological well-being of both sexes" (p. 152). Garbarino (1999) writes that androgyny is one of the major foundations for resilience in young boys: "The more successfully people incorporate both traditionally masculine and traditionally feminine attributes, the more likely they are to master the situations they face" (p. 169). Parents who are more androgynous are less likely to be stereotypical and more likely to offer a wider range of possible roles and behavior (Lindsey, 2106).

Gender-nonconforming children suffer early as a result of social labeling; the negative consequences serve to perpetuate rigid gender expectations. In many countries, young boys are accused of "acting like a girl" if they engage in a behavior considered inappropriate for a male. Labels like "pink boy" and "sissy" are used to denigrate boys and men who behave in gender-nonconforming ways. Sissies occupy a stigmatized and vulnerable social position and are usually considered social misfits, especially by other boys (Brooks, 2000; Corbett, 1999; Lippa, 2005; Mallon, 1999c). "Tomboy" has been a popular term for gender-nonconforming girls but has a wider range of meanings than "sissy." "Tomboy" can be used as a derogatory or complimentary label. In Western countries, from the late 1500s through the mid-1900s, "tomboy" referred to females acting outside gender role expectations. Eventually it came to refer to females living a healthier lifestyle inclusive of exercising, eating well, and dressing sensibly. As a result, tomboyism has become more acceptable, except for the linking to lesbianism in the early 1900s. Since World War II, "tomboy" has lost much of its pejorative punch. Because it is often more socially acceptable to be a tomboy, it is important to contrast the differential treatment of boys who "act like girls" from girls who "act like boys." This occurs as a result of sexist attitudes that underlie the assumption that male is better than female.

GENDERED OPPRESSION

Many labels can be applied to the mechanisms that enforce gendered oppression—sexism, heterosexism, homophobia, transphobia. Sexism, homophobia, and heterosexism are powerful social forces that affect all social groups. Sexism, the preferential treatment of males over females by men, and misogyny, the hatred of females and femininity, underlie the oppression of individuals who are female, gender variant, or transgender and those who are LGB. Homophobia, the fear of and hostility toward gay and lesbian people, is a product of sexism and reinforces gender role expectations. Heterosexism, the assumption that everyone is and should be heterosexual, contributes to the stigma attached to individuals who do not conform to societal gender norm expectations. Heterosexist attitudes, or heterocentrism, are subtler and less visible than homophobia in the same way that white privilege is less visible than overt racism. It is harder to name, uncover, address, and, thus, change. These mindsets are developed and maintained through education, socialization, and language.

Sexism

Despite early religions with powerful female gods, and historical examples of women leaders and warriors, for most of history, women have been denied political, social, and economic rights. It was not until the 18th century that some women began to be granted the right to vote. For example, in 1718 in Sweden, women guild members were allowed to vote, although this right was rescinded and then reinstated in 1734 for all taxpaying women. New Zealand is recognized as the first country to allow all people to vote (1893). Women in the United States did not receive the vote until 1920 (see Zinn, 2015, for a thorough history), and women in the Kingdom of Saudi Arabia received the right to vote and run for election in 2015. Except for Vatican City (which has a complicated voting process), women can now vote in all countries.

Sexism describes the social, structural, cultural, economic, and political systems established to maintain power relationships that privilege men over women. Sexism is tied to the concept of patriarchy, "a social system in which structural differences in privilege, power, and authority are invested in masculinity" (Cranny-Francis, Waring, Stauropoulos, & Kirby, 2003, p. 15). Patriarchal power structures serve to keep men in dominant and privileged positions. The disadvantages experienced by women are created by and maintained through cultural beliefs and stereotypes that present narrow, distorted, and harmful images of women (Milkie, 2002).

Violence against women is a global issue (Lips, 2017). It embedded in patriarchal structures with consequences at the structural and personal levels. Our social systems and political and economic structures support and reinforce gendered violence through low wages; exclusion; lack of access to resources, including education and health care; and sanctioned violence (Menjivar, 2016). Many females are exposed to gender-based violence in the home and the community; and all women are controlled through the fear of violence. During times of violent conflict "the use of gender-based violence is an exacerbation of cultural and structural violence present before the war erupted—and present after a peace accord is signed, unless specific attention is given to women's particular experience" (Lederach & Lederach, 2010, p. 156). Sexual violence is higher in societies where violence is condoned and women's roles are not valued (Lips, 2017). As estimated by the United Nations, globally approximately 35% of women experience physical and/or sexual intimate partner or nonpartner violence. There are estimates that it could be as high as 70% in some nations (United Nations, n.d.).

Addressing violence against women requires engaging change at social and structural levels. As described by Lederach and Lederach (2010), "The fluidity of borders in the 21st century requires that the global community begin addressing the structural and cultural violence that lies at the heart of sexual violence—violence that moves fluidly across places of war and peace" (Lederach & Lederach, 2010, p. 156). This means transforming policies and attitudes that are patriarchal and place a low value on women and girls to policies that are respectful and inclusive, and value women as equal to men.

Economic Disparity

Women represent approximately half of the world's population. The vast majority live in developing regions, which carry a heavier burden of poverty and disease (United Nations, 2015). Globally, women have a lower participation rate in the labor force; 77% of men and 50% of women participate in the labor force (United Nations, 2015). Overall poverty is decreasing globally, but not for women. The percent of women living in extreme poverty is 70%; it has not decreased (Project Concern International, n.d.). Globally, women continue to have lower wages than men. This is particularly pronounced for female-headed, single-parent households, which have the highest rate of poverty. This has a significant impact on children (United Nations, 2015). Further, women have fewer legal rights than men in many countries. And it is reported that in 90% of the world's economies, women have at least one legal difference restricting their economic opportunities and independence. Conditions are improving in developing regions; the biggest gender gaps exist in Northern Africa, sub-Saharan Africa, and West Asia (United Nations, 2015).

The movement of women globally has increased in part due to the migration of women from developing countries to provide child and household care for working women in developed countries (Ehrenreich & Hochschild, 2016). As women in wealthy countries move into the workplace, women from poor nations migrate to fill the labor gap. The result is a gap in female labor and care back home (Ehrenreich & Hochschild, 2016). Women of color make up a large part of the "servant class" (Ehrenreich & Hochschild, 2016). Much of this labor shift is racialized: The vast majority of women who migrate to serve the needs of white individuals, families, and communities are women of color.

Economic globalization has had a negative impact on the progression of women's rights and at the same time has created spaces for organizing working women in ways that are antisystem (Moghadam, 2015). Still, the change is uneven (Wilson, 2013). Economic globalization has expanded female proletarianization. In developing countries women are prone to take low-wage factory positions. This trend is referred to as the marginalization of women or housewifeization (Moghadam, 2015). In China, feminist work is usually oriented toward marginalized communities, including laid-off workers, migrant women workers, domestic helpers, and women who do not have the economic resources to fight injustice.

Intersectionality

Women are both divided and interconnected by race, class, and national origin. Although race and ethnicity have historically been conceptualized as gender neutral, there are clear trends running counter to this view (Handrahan, 2002). Women and men both suffer from discrimination based on race, ethnicity, and country of origin; but these experiences differ according to gender. Women of color—African, Indigenous, Latina, and Asian—are some of the poorest groups in the world with the highest rates in developing countries. White women tend to earn more money than women of color in part because they tend to be able to stay in school longer than women of color. However, in the United States, women of color, except Asian women, are more than twice as likely to live in poverty; children of color, except Asian, are three times more likely to live in poverty; and female-headed, single-parent families are more likely to live in poverty (Tucker & Lowell, 2016). For foreign-born women, children, female-headed, single-parent families experience high rates of poverty; older women, particularly women of color and foreign-born women, experience higher rates of poverty; women with disabilities experience the highest rate of poverty (Tucker & Lowell, 2016).

Gendered oppression "operates with and through other systems of opportunity and oppression, which give rise to a variety of different, yet sometimes overlapping, gender experiences among women and among men" (Baca Zinn et al., 2016, p. 14). These oppressions are interlocking, mutually reinforcing, and based on dynamics of domination and subordination (Jenson, 1998). Lorde (1983) writes that "Oppression and the intolerance of difference come in all shapes and sizes and colors and sexualities. . . . If we truly intend to eliminate oppression and achieve human liberation, heterosexism and homophobia must be addressed" (p. 9). Gender is complicated by intersecting power systems (Baca Zinn et al., 2016). Gender, sex, and sexual orientation overlap, and people's experiences of these identities are made more complex by identities of race, ethnicity, ability, class, caste, age, nationality, and/or religion.

Transphobia

Transgenderphobia, or transphobia, is the fear and hatred of people who are transgender. It is similar to homophobia and is a major threat to the safety and well-being of transgender populations. Like homophobia, transphobia falls along a continuum ranging from disapproval to violence. Transgender people of color are most likely to experience violence, and most murders of transgender people occur as a result of the intersection of racism, sexism, and transphobia, meaning that most transgender murder victims are trans women of color (Bettcher, 2007; Lombardi & Bettcher, 2005). Increased risk and exposure to violence is linked to other identities, including race/ethnicity, socioeconomic status, occupation, ability, and age (United Nations Free and Equal, 2017).

Although discrimination based on gender identity is generally considered banned under international human rights law, discrimination is common and pervasive (United Nations, 2017). Trans people face discrimination in education, housing, employment, and health care (United Nations, 2017). A study of LGBT people in Santiago, Chile, found a third of the participants experienced discrimination. Transgender participants, however, reported the highest levels of discrimination and victimization. About three quarters had been ridiculed with 60% reporting threats (Barrientos, Silva, Catalan, Gómez, & Longuieira, 2010). The US National Transgender Discrimination Survey revealed that half of trans people experienced job discrimination and a quarter lost their employment, while a fifth experienced housing discrimination and three quarters were harassed (National Center for Transgender Equality, n.d.).

Global Action for Trans Equality reported on the number of transgender people murdered in 2015. Numbers reported were highest in Brazil (113) followed by the United States (22) and Colombia (20). They tracked the numbers of murders across the Americas, Europe, East Asia, and South Africa, though they were not reported proportionally. The Trans Murder Monitoring Project reported 1,612 murders across 62 countries between 2008 and 2014, noting that many were exceptionally brutal (Transgender Europe, n.d.). In a 2008 study in Europe, 79% of participants reported experiences of harassment and violence; a high rate of underreporting was noted (Transgender Europe, n.d.). High rates of suicide have also been found in Europe, Canada, and the United States. The lack of legal recognition is a major factor in limiting rights and condoning violence (Neela & Knight, 2016). The Human Rights Commission of New Zealand and the Australian Human Rights Commission documented the obstacles trans people face in their struggles to gain equality and obtain security and dignity (Seuffert, 2009).

Studies have indicated that transgender populations are at high risk for HIV (Jobson, Theron, Kaggwa, & Kim, 2012). Globally, the risk is reported to be 50 times higher than for the general population (Neela & Knight, 2016). Yet, due to inadequate research with transgender people, the knowledge needed to develop appropriate services and interventions is limited. Based on the documentation of this failure, the Global Fund to Fight AIDS, Tuberculosis, and Malaria is funding partnerships designed to respond from a human rights perspective. In an effort to be responsive to local need, the strategies of the projects are grounded within the context of the country of implementation (Seale et al., 2010).

Shifts are occurring. The Human Rights Watch reported that between 2012 and 2015, five countries (Argentina, Columbia, Denmark, Ireland, and Malta) enacted laws that provide legal recognition. Some countries have long provided recognition. In Southeast Asia, there has long been some recognition of diverse genders; and Pakistan and Nepal provide legal recognition of a third gender. New Zealand and Australia have an option of "unspecified" in their census. Still, for trans people, the lack of legal recognition of their gender identity can result in being arrested due to behavior criminalized in many countries such as dressing in the clothing of another gender or being involved with someone of their same-sex (United Nations Free and Equal, 2017).

Heterosexism and Homophobia

Heterosexism centers heterosexual behavior as normal and stigmatizes homosexual and bisexual behavior; this is often reinforced through institutionalized prejudice and discrimination (Garnets, 2002; Herek, 1998; Lindsey, 2016). Because "heterosexuality is taken for granted" (Moi, 1999, p. 12), LGB people suffer the oppression of invisibility and secrecy. Heterosexism, the assumption that heterosexuality is normal and favored, "fuels homophobia, the fear and intolerance of homosexuals . . . and homosexuality" (Lindsey, 2016, p. 293). The assumption that marriage should be between a man and a woman is one example of heterosexism.

Homophobia is used to enforce sexism by keeping women and men in rigid sex roles. The fear that many people have of being labeled lesbian or gay, along with the concomitant discrimination, hatred, and violence fueled by homophobia, works to keep women's and men's behavior within the confines of that deemed acceptable by traditional gender role expectations. Political attacks on LGBT people are used to dismantle civil and human rights gains. Groups that oppose feminism and equality for women are often the same groups that speak out against lesbians and gay men (Faludi, 2006; Lindsey, 2016; Pharr, 1993, 1997).

Homophobia can result in many LGB individuals becoming fearful that they will lose friends, family, employment, and housing if they are honest about their sexual orientation. A life lived in secrecy out of fear of reprisal takes an emotional toll. Even worse are the consequences of homophobia that can lead to the loss of children to abuse and to suicide. The risk of suicide and the experience of violence are high for LGB youths.

There is ongoing resistance to efforts to address heterosexism and homophobia, alleviating the oppression of lesbians, gay men, and bisexuals. Neglecting the subject of homophobia allows heterosexuals to maintain their privilege (Smith, 1993). On a personal level, people may be afraid to fight for gay rights out of fear that others might think they are gay. Although homosexuality has not been viewed by the American Psychological

Association's *Diagnostic and Statistical Manual of Mental Illness (DSM)* as a mental illness since 1973, psychological, medical, child welfare, and other practice based on bias, lack of knowledge, and inadequate services are still prevalent (Hancock, 2000). Those committed to social and economic justice have a responsibility to dismantle all forms of oppression, including homophobia (Lorde, 1984, 2016).

Many people around the world use religion to support discrimination against LGB people. The three monotheistic Abrahamic religions (Judaism, Christianity, and Islam) all have a passage or two in their primary religious texts that are often interpreted to indicate that same-sex sexual activity between men is a sin. Although there are scholars in each of these religions that claim this is an inaccurate understanding of the texts, many followers of these religions fixate on this particular "sin" while ignoring other behavior that may be considered more egregious in their religion (such as adultery). Religious fundamentalists denigrate homosexuality and bisexuality and instill fear by persuading their constituents that LGB people are a threat to their marriages, families, and way of life. The current controversy raging around same-sex marriage is an example of how some followers of these religions promote rigid gender roles.

On the other hand, many religious traditions do not condemn same-sex sexual behavior. For example, in Hinduism, the Kama Sutra states that homosexual sex "is to be engaged in and enjoyed for its own sake as one of the arts" (Hinduism and Homosexuality, 2016). In both Buddhism and Taoism, sexual orientation is not specifically addressed; neither religion gives "homosexuality any . . . special status—positive or negative" (Human Rights Campaign, n.d., n.p.). Instead, "the expectation is not to harm, exploit or manipulate others" in any relationship (Human Rights Campaign, n.p.). Similarly, many followers of the three Abrahamic religions do not interpret their religious teachings as condemning LGB people or behavior (for further exploration, see David Helminiak on Christianity, Scott Siraj al-Haqq Kugle on Islam, and Joseph T. Farkasdi on Judaism).

FEMINISM: A MOVEMENT FOR CHANGE

Feminism is about ending all oppression, including gendered oppression. More specifically, it is

a) a belief that women all over the world face some form of oppression or exploitation, b) a commitment to uncover and understand what causes and sustains oppression, and c) a commitment to work individually and collectively in everyday life to end all forms of oppression, whether based on gender, class, race or culture. (Maguire, 1987, p. 5)

It is not anti-male. Nor is it a white women's movement, though, like all antioppression movements, it needs to be monitored for internal marginalization. In some Western countries, white women settled for suffrage for themselves and neglected suffrage for women and men of color. Likewise, men of color have settled for suffrage for themselves, neglecting suffrage for women. It is an ongoing struggle to work against racist, sexist, classist, heterosexist/homophobic marginalization.

People interested in a progressive agenda must work to end all oppression, including those at the intersections and at the margins. The social concerns that exist at the intersection of race/ethnicity, gender, and class have important implications for change (Dawson, 2001). According to Smith and Smith (1983),

> Feminism is the political theory and practice to free all women: women of color, working-class women, poor women, physically challenged women, lesbians, old women, as well as white economically privileged heterosexual women. Anything less than this is not feminism, but merely female self-aggrandizement. (p. 121)

Women are, however, divided by different worldviews created by race, ethnicity, nationality, caste, class, and sexual orientation. Although different worldviews have created blinders and divisions, they also have the potential to add depth to the women's movement.

Racial identity cannot be separated from gender, class, ethnicity, nationality, or sexual orientation. Women of color around the world have been major contributors to the development of feminist theory. These women helped emphasize the "negative impact that interactions between categories of identity, such as sexuality, race, class and gender, have on black women's lives" (White, 2001, p. 80). Black writers have also increased our awareness of the connection between race and sexuality (for example, Anne McClintock, bell hooks, Patricia Collins). Contemporary feminist studies is infused with examinations of diversity and difference (Baca Zinn et al., 2016).

Diversity feminism is a model that values the universal needs of women and girls while also centering the unique vulnerabilities and needs of indigenous women. Respect for the unique needs of indigenous women, who have been and continue to be harmed by the racist policies of settler nations, is centered along with a call for reconciliation. Certainly there are many nations impacted, including the United States, Canada, Australia, and New Zealand. Holistic analysis, which includes acknowledgment of structural and cultural patterns of violence that privilege some and marginalize others, recognizes the multifaceted complexity needed to engage innovative solutions grounded within a valuing of the unique context of each community. Transformative change requires self-determination and leadership inclusive of indigenous women and girls who face unique obstacles that universal models fail to recognize and address. Diversity feminism values the needs of all women while incorporating and centering women who have been marginalized by multiple intersecting dimensions, including race/ethnicity, gender, sexual orientation, economics, and nationality.

International, transnational, and global feminism bring the focus to issues faced by all women around the world: violence, poverty, and inequality. An early critique of transnational feminism was that it did not take into account "the specific nature of oppression as it occurs through the intersectionality of race, class, and other social-identity locations within a particular local context" (Moosa-Mitha & Ross-Sheriff, 2010, p. 107). Taking a global lens requires expanding the lens on feminist struggles to also include those of postcolonial, indigenous women. This requires analysis of colonialism and racial domination, and moving beyond the historical heterosexist bias of Western feminism (Spurlin, 2010).

On the sixtieth anniversary of the Universal Declaration of Human Rights, transnational feminist solidarity highlights the resistance of women across the globe at grassroots levels. "Transnational feminism is a theory and commitment to practice which recognizes differences and borders while building solidarity and transcending those borders" (Colling, 2010, n.p.). Linking feminism and human rights, which are antiracist and social justice oriented, creates the potential for transformative praxis (Collins et al., 2010). Mohanty (2003) calls for an antiracist feminist framework grounded in decolonization and dedicated to an anticapitalist critique. Transnational feminism has its roots in postcolonial theory. It emerged in part as the result of feminist networking around the United Nations agenda and engages both theory and activist practice. This connection is in part because of mutual opposition by the United Nations and transnational feminists to male domination, discrimination, and violence against women around the world.

CONCLUSION

The concepts of gender and sexual orientation, like race and ethnicity, are fluid across time and context. They are complex in their interactions and inextricably interconnected, gaining clarity as our lens moves to a global angle (Baca Zinn et al., 2016). Cultural and social contexts are connected to definitions, meanings, and behavior. This is true even as the history and manifestation of institutionalized oppression differ across race and ethnicity parallel to that of lesbians and gay men.

Women, people who are transgender, and people who are LGB fit Young's criteria for an oppressed group. They experience all five faces of oppression: exploitation, marginalization, powerlessness, cultural imperialism, and violence. In addition, the oppression of women interlocks with oppressions based on race, ethnicity, nationality, classism, gender identity, and sexual orientation. Women of color, along with lesbian and bisexual women, and lesbians of color experience impacts based on color, ethnicity, race, and sexual orientation that intensify exponentially with each additional oppressed identity.

The theoretical perspective of critical multiculturalism makes the point that none of the identities in the multicultural web stand alone. We cannot talk about gender, sex, and sexual orientation without talking about race, ethnicity, nationality, caste, and class. They are all part of the web of oppression. From this perspective, the study of gender and sexual orientation is not complete without an examination of the varied social locations and experiences of women, gay men, transgender, and intersex people. The interlocking systems of oppression, which affect individuals differently based on gender, sex, sexual orientation, race, ethnicity, nationality, caste, and class, "affect access to power and privileges, influence social relationships, construct meanings and shape people's everyday experience" (Ngan-ling, 1996, p. xix).

Questions for Consideration

Answer each of the following questions for your country or countries. Explore differences based on race, ethnicity, caste, ability, nationality, class, and religion for each of these questions.

1. What are the laws governing LGB and/or T behavior and rights?
2. How are females and males valued in relation to each other?
3. What are the patterns of education for women and men?
4. Who has access to health care and a healthy diet?
5. Who controls financial resources?

6. Are the lives and roles of women intrinsically valued?
7. Who serves in decision-making and leadership roles?
8. Who controls reproduction? How do women access sexual health services? Are women able to control the number and timing of the children they bear?
9. Are there gender differences in child custody, inheritance, and/or the passing of citizenship to one's children?

CHAPTER 5

People With Disabilities

Just as the dominant culture's ideal self requires the ideological figures of the woman to confirm its masculinity and of the black to assure its whiteness, so Emerson's atomized self demands an oppositional twin to secure its able-bodiness.

—R. J. Thomson, *Extraordinary Bodies*, 1997, p. 44

Like other social identities, disability is a socially constructed identity that can vary from country to country and one generation to another. The United Nations Convention on the Rights of People With Disabilities (CRPD) states:

> [D]isability results from the interaction between persons with impairments and attitudinal and environmental barriers that hinders their full and effective participation in society on an equal basis with others. (2006, n.p.)

This definition makes clear that it is not the "impairment" but rather the "barriers" that create a disability. For instance, people with mobility impairments may experience disability if they lives in a rural area without easy access to transportation. But for people who live in a city with a good mass transit system, the disability disappears (although not the mobility impairment). This social model sees disability as based in society, not in the body (World Health Organization [WHO], 2011).

The understanding of disability as a social construct helps explain the differences globally (a) in what is considered a disability (b) how disabilities are manifested, and (c) what is thought to be the cause of disabilities, from one culture to another. Although people with disabilities are often stigmatized in Western culture, some indigenous and aboriginal languages do not even have a word that translates as disability (Weaver, 2017). Ideas of mental health and mental illness occur in a cultural context with unique manifestations clearly associated with different cultures. Although not classified as a "culture-bound syndrome" in the *Diagnostic and Statistical Manual of Mental Disorders (DSM)*, dissociative identity disorder is found almost exclusively among Anglo-Americans (American Psychiatric Association, 2013; Paniagua, 2000). Similarly, koro, a fear of one's genitals retracting inside of one's body, is manifested primarily in China and other countries influenced by China (O'Neil, 2010).

> Many psychological anthropologists believe that the most meaningful criterion for defining mental illness is the degree of social conformity by an individual. People who are so severely psychologically disturbed and disoriented that they cannot normally participate in their society are universally defined as being mentally ill. (O'Neil, 2010, n.p.)

Those currently without an impairment are likely to become temporarily or permanently disabled during their lifetime with the risk increasing with age (Stroman, 2003; WHO, 2011). Global estimates on the number of people with disabilities range from 15.6% to 19.4% (WHO, 2011). Women, children with intellectual or sensory impairments, people with mental health or intellectual impairments, and people with the most severe impairments experience the most disadvantages (WHO, 2011). There are also certain countries and populations that experience higher prevalence of disabilities. For example, there are more people with disabilities

> . . . in lower income countries than in higher income countries. People from the poorest wealth quintile, women, and older people also have a higher prevalence of disability. People who have a low income, are out of work, or have low educational qualifications are at an increased risk of disability. . . .[C]hildren from poorer households and those in ethnic minority groups are at significantly higher risk of disability than other children. (WHO, 2011, p. 8)

Of course, disability does not just affect the person with the impairment but also the person's family and community.

Some impairments are present at birth; others are not. A person can become impaired/disabled in seconds with an accident or medical crisis. Impairment/disability can build over time, possibly resulting from or during a major medical or psychiatric illness. It may also result in an inability to work for long periods of time. The loss of income and change in socioeconomic status that often result may be life changing. For people who were not born with a disability but become disabled because of illness or injury, the shift from privilege to the oppression of disability can bring with it social isolation and economic hardship. It can be difficult to adjust to the isolation and stigmatization often experienced because of disability.

HISTORY

People with disabilities have a long diverse history in the way they have been perceived and treated across time and countries. Classical thinkers such as Aristotle established the definition of the perfect human body. People whose bodies did not meet the ideals of the perfect human body were described as deformed or deviant (Garland, 1995). Aristotle and Plato suggested that parents should not raise infants or children with disabilities but should abandon or kill them instead (Munyi, 2012); early Roman law admonished parents to kill children with disabilities.

Throughout history, many have thought a child was born with a disability because the child or the family was cursed or had done something wrong in a current or past life. Traditional Confucian beliefs in China or Hindu beliefs in India often explain disability as a punishment (Bjorn, 1990, as cited in Munyi, 2012; Rothman, 2003). During the 19th century, the moral model, according to which people with disabilities were seen as being punished for something they had done wrong, prevailed in the West (Rothman, 2003). Proponents of these beliefs provided charity to people with disabilities, although recipients had no right to expect anything and therefore needed to be grateful for whatever they received. These attitudes have not completely vanished.

Not all cultures stigmatized people with disabilities. In some cultures, there were no words for disability. Although this may suggest that disabilities were seen as a part of life, it does not indicate how people with disabilities were interacted with on a daily basis. This was exemplified in many communities (Munyi, 2012; Weaver, 2017). Several authors suggest that people with disabilities could be seen as a gift that brought good luck or kept away evil spirits.

There are several examples from the African continent. In reviewing these, it is important to keep the context in mind. Africa is the second largest and second most populous continent with 54 undisputed countries. There is wide diversity in language and cultural groups. European languages have increased the language diversity, and the impact of colonialism can be felt across the continent. Further, the population is growing rapidly, becoming increasingly young. It is important to keep this diversity and complexity in mind when highlighting examples. Although these are small communities, and their historical practices cannot be generalized, they can help us see possibilities.

Munyi (2012) reports great variability in attitudes toward people with disabilities. By way of example, there are communities in Kenya and Zimbabwe that view people with disabilities negatively; and in central Ghana, people with disabilities are viewed negatively by the Ashanti. This can be seen in the treatment of adults and children. In the Accra region of Ghana, however, people with intellectual disabilities are treated with kindness by the Ga. And people with disabilities are often seen as a gift by the Benin in West Africa and the Chagga in East Africa; they serve to keep evil spirits away. In northern Tanzania, the Chagga also think people with disabilities protect the community from evil spirits and therefore care for them. And in Kenya, the Turkana families care for children with disabilities who are considered to be a gift from God(s) (Munyi, 2012).

Eugenics

Davis (2016) posits that it is the idea of normalcy, not disability, which created the stigmatized view of people with disabilities as "less than." He notes that the word *normal* did not even enter the English language until around 1840. According to Davis, prior to the development of statistics and the creation of the idea of "normal as an imperative," the concept of the "ideal" or perfection was understood as unreachable by mere mortals (Davis, 2016, p. 2). Sir Francis Galton, a cousin of Darwin, focused on the idea of quartiles (four equal groups) to categorize human traits. In doing so, a hierarchy was created that divided people into categories from "below normal" to "above normal" (Davis, 2016). It is not seen as coincidental that Galton was also a eugenicist, that is, someone who wanted to perfect the human race. Darwin's idea of evolution suggested that the "best" of any species could be bred to eventually eliminate any "defects."

The ideas of Darwinism led to the eugenics movement—a scientific and social movement—in which the goal was to develop strategies to create the best genetic version of humans possible (see Bashford & Levine, 2010, for a more thorough discussion). This involved development and implementation of negative eugenics (for example, forced sterilization, forced abortions, antimiscegenation, and euthanasia) and positive eugenics (for example, education to encourage "fit" parents to have more children, tax incentives, and child stipends). The policies were designed to accomplish the goal of an "improved" human race. Inspired by the eugenics movement in the United States, in 1932, Germany passed its first law imposing forced sterilization on people with a "hereditary illness"; over 400,000 Germans, mainly people living in institutions, were sterilized. This was followed by so-called mercy killings of people deemed unworthy of life. Under Germany's T-4 program, 5,000 children were the first to be secretly euthanized with over 70,000 people murdered by the program's end in 1941 (Georgetown University, n.d.). The T-4 program was replaced by the Aktion 14f13 program, which killed over 6 million Jews and millions of others deemed "unworthy" (for example, people with disabilities, lesbians and gay men, African-Europeans) in concentration camps (Georgetown University, n.d.).

Holocaust?

Even in the 21st century the practice of eugenics is not a closed debate. Women and girls with disabilities are particularly vulnerable (Human Rights Watch, 2011c). Even though the Convention on the Rights of Persons With Disabilities provides protection, recognizing the right of women with disabilities to be safeguarded from forced sterilization, it is still debated and justified in many locations.

DISABILITIES IN THE UNITED STATES

The history of disabilities and disability policies in the United States is filled with federal legislation, lawsuits resulting in case law, activism, and the creation of schools and organizations to serve people with disabilities (for further reading, see Nielson, 2013; Trent, 2016; Pelka, 2012; among others). The Judeo-Christian values, philosophy, and traditions in the United Kingdom impacted the views and treatment of people with disabilities in the United States (Appleby, Colon, & Hamilton, 2010). The importance of individualism and work in this culture contributes to seeing people with impairments as less than others because they may require additional accommodations to function fully in society. Fortunately, the disabilities rights movement has brought the voices of people with disabilities into the mainstream in the United States, reminding us to do "nothing about us, without us" (United Nations, 2004).

From colonial times to the present, US laws (including case law) have both supported and oppressed people with disabilities. Social policy around disabilities has tended to focus on segregation, access (to education, employment, transportation, voting, etc.), services, and civil rights. For example, in *Buck v. Bell* (1927), the Supreme Court upheld the rights of states to force people with disabilities to be sterilized. Courts may still authorize the sterilization of people with disabilities who do not or cannot consent to the procedure if it is either what the person would want (based on their opinion prior to becoming disabled) or is in the person's best interest. On the other hand, laws have been adopted to ensure access and rights for people with disabilities. Many laws have been passed to ensure that children with disabilities are provided a free, public, appropriate education. Similarly, federal law now bans discrimination and requires "reasonable accommodations" that enable people with disabilities to have access to transportation, employment, voting, and so on.

Immigration laws in the United States have, at different times, banned immigration for people with certain disabilities. In 1896 immigrants who were "deaf, dumb, blind, idiotic, insane, pauper, and criminal" were not allowed to immigrate (Baynton, 2001, p. 47). In 1917, the list of disabilities that could be used to deny immigration grew to include ailments such as asthma, arthritis, flat feet, and varicose veins. Based on a 1949 court ruling (*United States v. Schwarz*, 1949), immigrants with mental illness could be refused entrance to the United States. In 1993, at the request of the National Institute of Health, the United States passed legislation prohibiting people living with HIV or AIDS from immigrating, or even entering the country for travel. This law remains in effect.

The so-called ugly laws of the 19th and 20th centuries (1840–1974) were a means of segregating people considered "diseased, maimed, mutilated or in any way deformed so as to be unsightly, disgusting or improper" from society (Thompson, 2011, p. 15; for a thorough discussion of the ugly laws, see Susan Schweik, 2009). Although these laws were primarily focused on beggars, the laws were used to keep people with disabilities out of sight of normal society. Both the eugenics movement and charity organization societies worked together to develop and enforce these laws. During this same time, the circus provided a space for the display of people with visible disabilities for the amusement and profit of others (Bogdan, 1988). These so-called freak shows flourished in Europe and North America from the mid-1800s to the mid-1900s. Although the last of the ugly laws in the United States was repealed in 1974, people continue to be discriminated against based on their appearance and impairments.

A more aware and humane social consciousness began to emerge after World Wars I and II (Appleby et al., 2001). After World War I, large numbers of veterans returned home with injuries. The government provided veterans, considered the worthy disabled, with rehabilitation services (Rothman, 2003). The Vocational Rehabilitation Act of 1920 was the first piece of federal legislation to address the issues of disabled veterans (Appleby et al., 2001). Most other people with disabilities still did not have access to resources (Rothman, 2003). World War II slowed the progress toward a more humane treatment of people with disabilities. With the end of the war, however, new federal legislation was introduced that responded to the needs of returning veterans exposed people to the horrors of the war: the Nazi medical experimentation on people with disabilities along with the extermination of 250,000 people with disabilities (Rothman, 2003).

There were many pieces of federal legislation passed during the 1900s that continue to be important in ensuring access, resources, and services for people with disabilities. One of the most important acts was the Social Security Act of 1935, which provided financial support for people who are elderly or blind, along with support for children with disabilities. Amendments to the Social Security Act in 1954 created Social Security Disability Insurance (SSDI), which supports workers who become disabled before the age of 65. In 1965, Medicaid and Medicare were created to provide medical insurance for workers who are elderly (over 65) or disabled. However, it was the Rehabilitation Act of 1973 that finally banned discrimination against persons with disabilities in any program that received federal funding. Then in 1975, the Education for All Handicapped Children Act was passed, requiring that all children with disabilities be provided services designed to meet their needs in a setting as close to a regular classroom as possible. It was due to the Americans With Disabilities Act (ADA) that was passed in 1990 that people with disabilities were provided broad civil rights. The ADA requires accommodations and bans discrimination in public transportation, toilets in private buildings, communication, and employment. Employers with more than 15 employees must provide "reasonable accommodations" that enable employees with disabilities to perform their job duties. Finally, the Mental Health Parity Act of 1996 requires that health insurers provide mental health coverage with no difference in annual or lifetime benefits when compared to other medical benefits.

In the United States, society's focus on perfection and beauty frequently results in excluding images of people with disabilities from the media. Historically people with disabilities have been portrayed as either victims (Tiny Tim in *A Christmas Carol*), heroes (Matt Murdock in the film *Daredevil*), inspiring (Helen Keller), or as villains (Captain Hook in *Peter Pan*), rather than as rounded individuals. However, since the 1990s, the number of advertisements, television shows, and movies featuring characters with disabilities has increased, although these are still generally attractive people with nondisfiguring disabilities; and they are often played by people without disabilities. Nonetheless, with advocacy from disability rights groups regarding media images, there has been some improvement in recent portrayals. For example, the characters Walter Junior (*Breaking Bad*) and Doctor Fife (*Private Practice*) are both played by actors with disabilities about characters whose disabilities are part of who they are but do not define them. Similarly, BBC's *The Office* was produced by a person with disabilities and includes a character with disabilities played by an actor with disabilities. People who use wheelchairs have appeared in television and print advertisements for companies such as McDonald's, Nike, Levi's, and Target. There is a significant market among people with disabilities over the age of 15, who have an estimated income of $700 billion with discretionary funds (Bauman, 2005).

In conclusion, the history of the treatment of people with disabilities in the United States has generally moved from the exclusion and segregation of people with disabilities to the adoption of laws banning discrimination against people with disabilities. However, as of 2017, the United States has yet to ratify the Convention on the Rights of People With Disabilities.

Indigenous Populations in the United States and Disabilities

In contrast to dominant Western cultures that emphasize individualism, in general, indigenous and aboriginal belief systems are more interdependent and balance focused within the whole community (and nature). Although one must not overgeneralize about Native American and Alaskan Native people in the United States, since there are over 560 tribes and 2,000 languages spoken among them, "in general, indigenous philosophies and belief systems are typically inclusive and recognize people with disabilities as community members, relations and people who are part of the balance of all elements of creation" (Weaver, 2017, p. 1). The focus is, instead, on the "gifts the person [with disabilities] brings, not on their deficits" (Weaver, 2017, p. 7). Native Americans focus on wellness, which includes balance, harmony, life forces, and interconnectedness (Cross & Day, 2017; Weaver, 2017). Wellness is about balance between self and life forces that are holistic rather than fragmented. This is a context in which Native American people with disabilities "are typically valued for what they bring to their families, communities and nations" (Weaver, 2017, p. 1), not on deficits of the body (see Weaver, 2017, for a more thorough discussion about Native Americans and disabilities).

Native American/Alaskan Native peoples have much higher rates of disabilities, poverty, and exposure to environmental toxins and violence than others in the United States (Weaver, 2017). They experience two to three times more chronic disease and earlier onset of disabilities (Moss, Schell, & Goins, 2006). Among those older than 65, they experience higher rates of disabilities: 57.6% have disabilities compared to 41.9% of the non-Native population (Moss et al., 2006). Similarly, Native American/Alaskan

Native children are overrepresented in special education. According to Faircloth (2006), Native American/Alaskan Native children comprise about 1% of children in school, but 1.5% of children in special education. In Bureau of Indian Affairs (BIA) schools, 17% of children are in special education.

Due to the unique status of Native American/Alaskan Native tribes as sovereign nations within the United States based on various treaties, laws, and Supreme Court and other court decisions, the government of the United States has agreed to accept a unique responsibility to Native American/Alaskan Native peoples for health services (Weaver, 2017). Currently, the Indian Health Services (IHS) within the US Department of Health and Human Services is responsible for serving Native American/Alaskan Native peoples, primarily through poorly funded services on or near Indian country. It is important to note that these services are not a form of insurance, nor an entitlement; they are subject to discretionary funding as allocated by Congress. As noted in testimony before the US Commission on Civil Rights, IHS Director Dr. Charles Grim stated that IHS is a program of "universal eligibility but limited availability" (US Commission on Civil Rights, 2004, p. 49).

The federal government funded health care for all Native Americans in 1832 as one means of assimilating "Native Americans into the general population by emphasizing Western medicine over traditional healing practices" (US Commission on Civil Rights, 2004, p. 48). Yet today when Native American/Alaskan Native peoples look for healing, they often first turn to family members, grandparents, and spiritual resources (Begay, et al., 1999; Cross & Day, 2017; Weaver, 2017). Unfortunately, on top of all the other atrocities experienced at the hands of colonists, many traditional Native American/Alaskan Native healing ceremonies were made illegal in the United States until the passage of the American Indian Religious Freedom Act (AIRFA) of 1978. Until that time, drumming, dancing, and possession of eagle feathers and peyote were banned in many states. Unfortunately, many sacred sites have been decimated or used for other purposes by the US government.

DISABILITIES IN INDIA

To understand disability in India, one must consider the country's history of diverse religions, caste systems, and colonization. These variables create a different understanding of, and response to, impairments. In traditional Indian society, people with impairments usually lived/live with their families and were/are not hidden away in institutions (Chandra, 2015). This is because caring for others in the extended, or joint, family is considered a shared responsibility. This care promoted/promotes lifelong social and financial support for all members of the family, each contributing as they are able (Chandra, 2015). Unlike the United States, India signed and ratified the Convention on the Rights of People With Disabilities in 2007.

As noted, the religions of India impact understanding of impairments and disabilities. Hinduism, the oldest religion in the world, started in India, where it remains the dharma of almost 80% of the population (Central Intelligence Agency [CIA], 2017). And Buddhism, another religion that originated in India, experienced centuries of popularity in India. These two religions have great influence on the understanding of disability in India. In both religions, providing respect and care for people with impairments is expected. Both religions also suggest that a person's disability may be the result of karma from bad deeds in a past life. On the other hand, karma can also result in helpers being placed in a person's life when the person experiences a disability, indicating good deeds done in past lives merit support in this life.

The caste system as it exists today in India is a result of British colonial rule (Dirks, 2001). Under British rule, the once fluid caste system became a strict hierarchy with some castes being identified as criminals and others privileged (Dirks). Although today discrimination based on caste is illegal, caste is correlated with the prevalence of disabilities, the impact of impairments and the response people with disabilities receive. Both male and female Dalits (referred to Scheduled Castes in the Indian constitution) have 1.5 times more disabilities than others (Saikia, Bora, Jasilonis & Shkolnikov, 2016). Being a Dalit increases likelihood of disability "because of poor hygiene, living conditions including malnutrition, inaccessibility to health care and dangerous working conditions" (Mehrotra, 2013, p. 301). In addition, the majority of Dalits live in rural areas of India where access to services, health care, education and transportation is limited therefore the impact of an impairment is more debilitating (Mehrotra).

Colonization impacted understanding of impairments and disabilities in India. Although India has centuries of home rule to its history, it also experienced centuries of rule and colonization by Arabs, Turkish slaves, the Mongol Empire, Portuguese, French, and finally, Great Britain. Unfortunately, over the last two millennia, colonization took India from an advanced civilization with no slavery, extensive sanitation and water systems, and an organized education system to a country depleted of wealth, where 41% of urban residents do not have adequate sanitation (Water Aid, 2016), 39% of children under age 5 are undernourished (International

Food Policy Research Institute, 2015), and most people live in debt bondage (Knight, 2012). Although the Indian economy is one of the fastest growing in the world, the colonial drain of Indian wealth impacts the ability of the country to provide adequate services for people with disabilities. For example, although the 1995 Persons With Disabilities Act calls for a wide array of educational and vocational services for children with disabilities, the availability of these services depends on the state's economic capacity and development.

OPPRESSION OF PEOPLE WITH DISABILITIES

Many people with disabilities live in conflict settings or in developing countries, where they experience a range of barriers to education, health care and other basic services. In many countries, they are subjected to violence and discrimination. People with disabilities are also often deprived of their right to live independently, as many are locked up in institutions, shackled, or cycled through the criminal justice system. Many of these human rights abuses are a result of entrenched stigma and a lack of community-based services essential to ensuring their rights.

—*Human Rights Watch, 2010a, n.p.*

The oppression of people with disabilities, like that experienced by other oppressed groups, is both active and passive, resulting from structural factors and from "the fact that this structure is not questioned" (Northway, 1997, p. 738). Historically, the concept of disability has often been used to marginalize women, people of color, and immigrants by supporting the claim that they are unfit for full citizenship (Kudlick, 2003). Likewise, homosexuality was considered a mental disorder in the United States until 1974. And slavery in the West was often justified by the supposition that Africans lacked sufficient intelligence to participate in society on an equal basis. As another example, in the West, people from Mongolia, like many other nationalities, were believed to be intellectually inferior (Tarek, 2005). When John Langdon Down, a physician from England who worked at an institution for children with developmental disabilities, noticed physical similarities among one group of the children who he thought looked like people from Mongolia, he labeled the children as "Mongoloids" (Tarek, 2005).

Young's five faces of oppression (exploitation, marginalization, powerlessness, cultural imperialism, and violence) can be applied to the oppression experienced by people with disabilities. The oppression to which people with disabilities are subjected may be compounded by other forms of oppression. In a system of overlapping oppressions, women with iden-tifiable disabilities, like women of color, have been marginalized economi-cally, socially, and politically. There are parallels between the value assigned to female bodies and those attributed to disabled bodies (Thomson, 1997). The bodies of people who are physically impaired, as well as those of women and people of color, have been labeled by society as inferior and deviant.

The dehumanization of people with disabilities leads to physical vi-olence and social isolation. People who are visibly physically or mentally disabled experience a high rate of overt and covert violence. This violence is related to cultural imperialism. Cultural imperialism, which establishes able-bodiedness as the cultural norm, creates an environment in which people with disabilities are exploited and marginalized (Michalko, 2002; Thomson, 1997). When measured against the "norm," difference is usually seen as less than (Northway, 1997). Because of ableism, the defining of people with disabilities in a negative and stereotypical manner, individuals with disabilities are often perceived as deficient or deviant; many people be-lieve that they lead less fulfilling lives (Holland Bloorview Hospital, 2016).

Able-bodiedness is often seen as the natural state; if one is not able-bodied, then one is different or defective and therefore the "other." The negative perceptions held about people with visible disabilities result in prejudice and discrimination. This negative view is often internalized by people with disabilities, including the idea of a "hierarchy of disability" in which some disabilities are considered more acceptable than others (Snow, 2016). Although perceptions about people with less visible disabilities may not be as negative as those held about people with more visible disabilities, they can nonetheless affect daily living and the long-range opportunities of people with disabilities. For example, skeptical educational personnel may fail to provide appropriate accommodations and resources for those with learning disabilities because they are less visible.

The marginalization of people with disabilities is further enabled by poorly supported education, inadequate and exploitative employment, so-cial stigma, misdirected health policy, and limited political resources. The physical environment serves to maintain marginalization. Many people be-lieve that persons with disabilities do not have the power to determine their own needs or achieve their goals. Individuals with disabilities are under-represented in professional and management positions; conversely, they are overrepresented in low-skilled, poorly paid, and less secure positions (WHO, 2011). People with disabilities are too often sidelined in the labor force; they experience high rates of unemployment, in part due to social isolation which limits access to the labor market. This is not only because of limitations employers perceive in people with disabilities but also from educational systems that marginalize and fail to meet the needs of people with disabilities.

FINAL THOUGHTS

The fields that took up the challenge of studying race, gender, and sexuality provide valuable analytic and theoretical tools for exploring disabilities, which has often been left out of antioppression analysis (Kudlick, 2003). Current-day, Western disability studies generally rejects using a pathology-based medical model through which to view disability, and instead it views disabilities as social categories informed by social interactions. Critical disability studies remind us that disability is "entangled with other forms of oppression and revolutionary responses" (Goodley, 2012, p. 631).

The disabilities rights movements around the world have had some success in educating people about people with disabilities, correcting inaccurate stereotypes, supporting important legislation, and ensuring access to a broad range of services. Approaching disability as a social category rather than as an individual attribute allows society to move the discussion and responsibility for change into a more open arena; and it allows the public to see the responsibility for change not just as a matter of interest to people in rehabilitation, special education, and related fields (Kudlick, 2003). Communities and organizations have the opportunity and obligation to provide the resources necessary for everyone, including those living with disabilities, to reach their fullest potential.

Questions for Consideration

1. How are people with disabilities treated in your country/culture?
2. What is the history of people with disabilities in your country/culture?
3. What national policies support or hinder the inclusion of people with disabilities in education, the workplace, political life, and/or other parts of society?
4. What resources are available for people with disabilities? This might include financial assistance, housing, and health care. Is health care considered a right or an entitlement?

CHAPTER 6

Intersectionality

Positioning Privilege and Marginalization

It is not difference which immobilizes us, but silence. And there are so many silences to be broken.

—Audre Lorde, *Sister Outsider*, 2007, p. 44

Identity can't be compartmentalized. You can't divide it up into halves or thirds or any other separate segments. I haven't got several identities: I've got just one, made up of many components in a mixture that is unique to me, just as other people's identity is unique to them as individuals.

—Amin Maaloof, *In the Name of Identity: Violence and the Need to Belong*, 2012, p. 2

The groundwork has been laid for the exploration of groups and communities that have been marginalized and systemically oppressed. Critical multiculturalism and Young's five faces of oppression provide a theoretical framework for examination and evaluation. Critical self-reflection integrated with historical, political, and developmental knowledge building provide a base for creating a framework for change. Race, ethnicity, nationality, caste, class, and color; gender, sex, and sexual orientation; and ability status as examined through the theoretical lens of critical multiculturalism and further intersected with religion, age, and socioeconomic status highlight the complexity.

Each of us holds a multiplicity of identities, some of which are used to justify oppressing some while granting privileges to others (May, 2015). A person's identity encompasses more than just the dimensions considered in models of individual development over the life span. Name, history, social status, gender and sex, ethnoracial identity, sexual orientation, ability status, income/socioeconomic status, caste, education, and religion all come into play. It is our identities, and their association with certain attributes, stereotypes, and norms, that often define how others see us. Intersecting identities are not separate wherein one dimension can just be added onto the other. Their impact is exponential as they fuse together into a whole. A Latina faces levels of marginalization that go beyond being female and being Latina. She faces a unique set of oppressions because her identities are fused into "Latina."

The intertwining and overlapping mechanisms of oppression that impact historically marginalized groups have a unique history and dynamic. This provides a base of knowledge for exploration that supports learning and living intersectionally. Within intersectionality, "lived identities are treated as interlaced and systems of oppression as enmeshed and mutually reinforcing: one form of identity or inequality is not seen as separable or subordinate" (May, 2015, p. ix). The oppression of each group of people operates differently, but not separately. Failing to use the lens of intersectionality creates a false picture by not taking into account the multiple layers and forms of oppression experienced by people. Developing a full understanding of identity and oppression requires recognizing the ways multiple identities are enmeshed and, therefore, need to be addressed simultaneously without the subordination of one identity over the other (May, 2015). bell hooks (2006, 2015) uses the phrase "white supremacy capitalist patriarchy" to go beyond using a single-focused gendered or racial lens, reminding us of the "interlocking systems of domination" (n.p.). She uses the term *white supremacy* over *racism* because

> racism in and of itself did not really allow for a discourse of colonization and decolonization, the recognition of the internalized racism within people of color and it was always keeping things at a level at which whiteness and white people remained at the center of the discussion. (hooks, 2006, n.p.)

Globally, race, ethnicity, tribal affiliation, religion, color, gender and sex, caste, class, and nationality can each be the master status by which people are judged. This master status then informs a social order and socioeconomic status because of structures that intentionally, or unintentionally, are put in place to provide opportunities for those with privilege and limit those without privilege in a particular society. As we can see in Teresa's story, positional status can shift with a change in location and with it one's experience of oppression and privilege (Box 6.1).

Box 6.1
TERESA: LOCATION AND IDENTITY

My name is Teresa, and I immigrated from Venezuela to the United Kingdom with a student visa. I knew when I was 5 years old that I wanted to attend college in the United Kingdom, although there were no girls in my extended family or my community who did so. I just knew it could be done. My family is considered upper middle class, my mother is mestizo (mixed race), and my father is white. He is a well-respected architect. I received a private school education where I studied English in preparation for my British education. I attended school with other kids who looked just like me. I had little contact with people of the darker hue except for the service people who worked for my family. Growing up, I never gave it much thought of what their lives were like or why we were privileged and they were not.

I applied to 25 colleges in the United Kingdom and received many offers. I was fortunate to receive a full 4-year scholarship to a prestigious university. I had vacationed with my family in the United Kingdom and Europe several times, and I was confident that moving to the United Kingdom would just take a little adjustment. I never gave much thought to my identity because it was never called into question: I was a white Venezuelan. As soon as I arrived on campus, I was supplied with much information and recommendations on student groups to join. The one that caught my attention was for a Latina women's group. So I thought, this is great, I can meet women who are just like me.

I attended the first meeting, and I was surprised to see women of every shade and hue, straight hair, curly and kinky hair; and I thought I might have gotten the wrong room number. We all introduced ourselves and many spoke with strong accents and some spoke broken English. I felt proud that I had taken English classes for 12 years and spoke the language impeccably, or so I thought. There were 25 of us and most of the women were first, second, and third generation born in the United Kingdom, and 10 of us were born elsewhere. For most of us, English was our second language, but some of the women spoke no Spanish at all. Still, we had no difficulty communicating with each other.

In my home community everyone treated me and my family with respect, but no one knows me here. I soon learned that being upper class in Venezuela has no meaning here—no polite greetings, no special invitations; and I learned that I must spend my money carefully because things are so much more expensive. Yet what was most troubling is that Latina women are often asked to explain themselves, whether from the United Kingdom or not. They assume we are all from the same country— Brazil, even though they speak Portuguese and not Spanish—and ask if we know how to salsa—which is from Cuba—and if we've been to Carnival in Rio de Janiero. If we speak with an accent different from their own, we are often spoken to as children, followed by "Do you understand?" This is not just the other students; some teachers do these things as well. I do have to admit that sometimes the slang and common language that some people use do leave me confused. Some of the men think that Latinas are hot for men from the United Kingdom and are fair game because we are desperate to get a green card.

Being in a place where you are the "other" can be frustrating and exhausting, so we find comfort with each other either at the dining hall, where we all sit together speaking Spanish, or when the weather is nice, we meet on the quad and share our stories and frustrations. Even these acts of self-care bring suspicion—Are they talking about us and why can't they all speak English?

Context informed Teresa's access to privilege and the ways she was marginalized based on identity as a Latina. The attitudes in the United Kingdom were framed by the Protestant belief in the myth that success is based on individual merit. That is, those who work hard succeed. A quick examination of the policies that deny or limit access and the impact of pervasive poverty and structural barriers undermines this myth. Nonetheless, this myth limits the ability of people with privilege to see the barriers obstructing people in the "marginalized" categories. They assume they deserve their success because of their own hard work, not because they went to better funded schools, had more access to resources, or speak with an accent similar to the potential employer.

Oppressions occur on a multilevel playing field that is not equal for all players (Taylor, 2009). Although people of color make up more than two thirds of the world population, the wealth resides in the hands of a few people and countries (Oxfam, 2016), the majority of whom are white, Western men. Sixty-two people (majority white, Western, and male) have more wealth than the poorest 50% of the world; and the 1% richest people own more than the other 99% of the world's people (Oxfam, 2016). Approximately one third of the world's population lacks basic sanitation, 15% lack access to clean water, 15% cannot read or sign their name, and 11% are undernourished (World Bank Group, 2016). The creation of divisions between groups encourages competition rather than collaboration, privileging those with systemic access and resources.

INTERSECTING IDENTITIES

Understanding people individually and collectively requires us to weave together the privilege and marginalization continuums. Feminist, critical race, and other critical theories examine the oppression faced by women and other marginalized communities (Appleby, Colon & Hamilton, 2010). These theories provide a context for understanding the role of both social constraints and opportunities in shaping lives (Garnets & Peplau, 2001). It is important to be aware of, and sensitive to, the issues faced by different groups. These issues have an effect on daily living, personal and collective adjustment, access to resources, and coping mechanisms. It is important to recognize that diversity exists both between and within identities (Lum, 2010). It is within the diversity of worldviews that the potential for personal and human growth exists.

The intersectionality model illustrates the distinctions between and across forms of oppression and privilege (for further discussion, see Baines, 2000; Crenshaw, 1989, 1991, 2014; Mullaly, 2002, 2010). The faces of oppression are applied across identities even if they vary in expression across individuals and communities. The intersections add to the complexity of identity, the experience of oppressions, and access to privileges. Individuals may be oppressed in one identity, but privileged in another. The privilege of whiteness may be mitigated by a person's ability status, which leads to lack of access to educational and economic resources. Similarly, the relative value or importance of a particular identity may be different from one country to another. A Qatari may experience privilege in the Arab Gulf because of their nationality, but oppression in Europe or the United States because of their ethnicity, nationality, and religion. See the Web in Figure 6.1, which depicts intersectionality through the inclusion of multiple identities.

The identity categories covered in the Web can be used to reflect on systemic and structural dimensions that enforce power dynamics underlying community relationships. The groups in the center are those that usually have institutionalized privilege, whereas those further outside the center usually do not. However, within each wedge outside the center, placement of an identity in the illustration is random and does represent distance from privilege and resources. For instance, lesbians are not necessarily more oppressed than bisexuals; it depends on the context. Someone who identifies as bisexual may experience more discrimination in the lesbian, gay, and bisexual community, but less among heterosexuals.

The complexity often lies at the intersections. Those intersections hold points of friction or conflict; at the same time, they hold the potential for transformative change and keys to resilience. Kajaly's story (see Box 6.2) is one that balances at the intersection of national origin, ethnoracial identity, gender, religion, and sexual orientation as they further intersect with education.

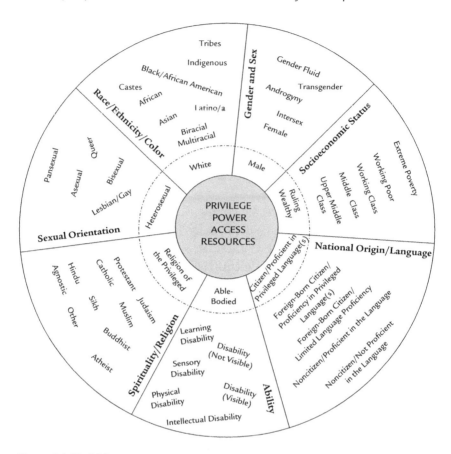

Figure 6.1: The Web.

Kajaly has the strengths of social connection through his family, friends, community, and religion. He also has the strength of temperament, cognitive ability, and education. Due to these personal, interpersonal, and community strengths, he has a resilience that supports his growth. How can this resilience now be used to help him transition to integrate new, intercultural connections that may require shifting family traditions and norms?

People's internalized views of what is normal lead to assumptions about individuals and groups. For instance, many people who are white in the United States may assume that all African Americans come from a background of poverty. In fact, the majority of African Americans do not live in poverty. Middle-class status can alleviate some of the negative

---

Box 6.2
KAJALY: INTERSECTIONALITY, RISK, AND RESILIENCE

Kajaly and his family immigrated to the United States from Gambia when he was 5 years old. Like most immigrants, his parents were seeking better opportunities for their children. Although it was a heart-wrenching decision to leave their home country, there were limited opportunities for their children to get a good education. Kajaly and his two older sisters attended public schools in their North Carolina community.

He is currently in his junior year at the university. Kajaly says that he has learned a great deal about the difficulties of being Muslim in a secular world and wants to be able to help children, youth, and young adults navigate Western culture while embracing Islam. He has become accustomed to the "Western" ways of doing things, has many non-Muslim friends, and has also remained strong in his Islamic faith. Kajaly believes in Allah and the Prophet Muhammad, engages in salat (prayer) five times a day, practices Zakat (donating to the poor and needy), observes Ramadan (fasting), and plans Hajj (pilgrimage to Mecca) sometime in the future.

Although Kajaly feels comfortable as a US citizen, he is conflicted and concerned about losing his way. He is devoted to his parents and does not want to disappoint them because he knows they have sacrificed so much for him and his sisters. He has an interest in a woman who is African American and not Muslim. Both have struggled to attend university while working part-time jobs to pay for their expenses. Her family has a good reputation. This match can be permitted if she believes in Christianity or Judaism. Like many Muslim families, Kajaly's family does allow dating. He has not spoken to his parents because he fears they may not consider this a suitable match and therefore may not approve. Islam also teaches that life is a test and one must show one's devotion to Islam no matter how difficult.

---

effects of ethnoracial oppression by providing access to resources such as health care, housing, education, childcare, and transportation (Mullaly, 2010).

One's location in the social order often determines one's access to power and resources. In the Web, those in the center usually have more access to resources than those outside the center. As you look at the wheel, think about the ways in which power and resources are distributed in your country, based on identity. For example, to understand the impact of privilege for men compared to the oppression of women in your country, compare variables such as poverty rates, literacy rates, and educational achievement between men and women. To examine the impact of privilege and oppression at the intersection of gender and disability, compare those same variables between men without a disability, women without a disability, men with a disability, and women with a disability. Through this process, the impact of oppression and privilege can be recognized.

In the same way that the intersecting dimensions of oppression overlap, so do the mechanisms used to maintain oppression and privilege. Individuals who are part of marginalized communities are affected by exploitation, marginalization, powerlessness, cultural imperialism, and violence (Young, 2004), yet the forms these mechanisms take may vary. For instance, LBGT populations in many countries must remain hidden or face abuse, arrest, and/or even death. The hiding is part of the oppression.

These mechanisms and the enforcement of oppressions are the means for structuring and maintaining inequality. Social and economic systems exploit some groups, thus keeping them marginalized. In employment, education, housing, and health care, some groups are privileged while others experience the marginalization that comes from oppression. Cultural violence is used to maintain structural and physical violence (Galtung, 1990). Cultural violence overtly or covertly centers the privileged group as "normal" and sees other groups as the "other." Mechanisms of violence and intimidation (cultural violence) frighten and reinforce oppression, causing people, family, and community to impose limitations on themselves. For instance, women monitor their behavior and limit their movement because of the fear of rape. This is a cultural concern for the individual and also a fear that affects all women because social structures fail to take the necessary actions to seriously and effectively respond to rape. Dismantling the mechanisms of oppression requires working together rather than in isolation. The interplay between the cultural, social, and economic systems makes it necessary to engage in multilevel change.

Positionality

The Web provides a model for examining one's position at the intersections of class, caste, sex and gender, race/ethnicity, color, religion, ability, nationality, and sexual orientation. Exploration of these intersections and Maher and Tetreatult's (1993) positionality are aids for developing an understanding of oppression. Positionality is "determined by where one stands in relation to the 'other'" (Merriam et al., 2001, p. 411). It is a theory that incorporates the impact that overlapping identities have on how people create meaning (Kezar, 2002). People make meaning based on the complex web of identities and one's position in relationship to systemic structures that provide or limit access to political, economic, and organizational power. Positionality influences access to social, political, educational, health care, and economic opportunities. Age, class, religion, and national origin intersect with sex, gender, ethnicity, race, ability, and sexual orientation. Positionality adds to other theories on identity development that explore this complexity and the impact of intersecting identities.

Age intersects across identities and contexts; and, as it shifts, it can change a person's positionality. Changes in social environment, income, and/or health, or loss of loved ones can result in immediate reshifting of position. Older adults experience discrimination and bias in most individualistic societies. In the United States, adults 29–60 are generally the ones with privilege and power. As one ages, women lose status younger than men; and older men in the top 20% socioeconomic status tend to hold power. As you view the Web, consider the other diversities coupled with age identity. Not all older adults are disabled; in spite of this, they are often viewed through this lens. What might be the positionality for an older Asian gay man? How might an older black woman be positioned?

Each of us is positioned in a particular context in terms of race, ethnicity, color, class, caste, gender and sex, nationality, religion, and ability at our birth. One's position at birth is not a matter of choice. Positions within and across multiple identities provide an indicator of a person's status. Identities can change over time (i.e., religion, ability, nationality, gender, sexual orientation, age), creating the potential for transitions.

When positioned in a place of privilege, a person's vision can be limited. Privilege often affects a person's internalized assumption of normality; this can impede a person's ability to see obstacles faced by those with an oppressed identity. For instance, in regard to sexual orientation, heterosexuality has typically been viewed as the "normal" sexual orientation. This results in the assumption that all others are not normal. For example, if we see a couple we assume to be heterosexual holding hands, we think little or nothing of it in most countries; however, if we see a couple we assume to be lesbian or gay holding hands, we may be offended at the public display of affection. Nationality can change the interpretation. For instance, in Arabian Gulf countries (Kingdom of Saudi Arabia, Qatar, United Arab Emirates, Oman, Kuwait, Bahrain, and Yemen), two women or two men holding hands is not a statement of sexuality. It is about friendship, family, and closeness. If we cannot see the impacts the assumptions about normality create for people, then we limit our ability to observe and envision beyond what we consider to be the "norm." When people with privilege

Box 6.3

INTERSECTIONALITY IN HEALTH CARE

Yolanda is a 40-year-old woman who was born in Puerto Rico but is now living in a large urban community in the mainland United States where many other Latino/Latina families live. She has a good command of the English language but still speaks with what would be considered an accent by the people around her. She works in retail sales at a large department store, and her employer provides health insurance, for which she is very thankful. Without the assistance of her employer, she would not be able to afford health insurance on her own. Yolanda also works a night shift cleaning office buildings several days a week. Although she loves her day job, her salary does not cover all of her expenses, rent, utilities, groceries, and so on. She has sought and has been offered other jobs that pay more, but there is either no health insurance or the employer pays only a fraction of the cost. Although her day job offers health insurance, she does not receive paid sick days, so when she is not feeling well, she pushes on at work.

When Yolanda went to urgent care with a high fever and other unspeci-fied complaints, it was because her employer would not let her work when she was visibly sick and sent her home. She had never used her health in-surance and did not have a primary care doctor, so urgent care was her only option. It would take three bus transfers to get to the nearest clinic, which was in a predominantly white community and about an hour and thirty minutes travel time. At the registration desk, she was asked to show proof of insurance and identification. "I'm sorry I didn't hear what you asked of me . . . can you please repeat the question?" The clerk paused and then asked her where was she from and asked if she were legal. The clerk stated that they get too many people like me who don't pay. Yolanda countered, "I have health insurance and I am from Puerto Rico and therefore I am a citizen." The clerk stated that there was a copayment she must pay before she could see a doctor, and she needed to prove that she could pay it be-fore completing the registration. Yolanda handed her a credit card. "Will this do?" The clerk asked for two picture IDs, and Yolanda showed her picture badge from the well-known department store and her driver's li-cense. The clerk's tone cooled and she completed the registration.

While Yolanda was waiting to see the doctor, she was praying that she didn't have to miss anymore work. She has always been careful with her finances, but she does not earn enough with her two jobs to save more than a few dollars a month. "I had been using teas and herbal remedies that I was taught to make as a child. Everyone in my village would come to my mother's small house to be healed; she was the local healer. I have since accepted that there is a place for Western medicine but our local ways of healing have many benefits as well."

"I was fortunate to get a doctor who has spent many summers providing medical care in developing countries. The doctor carefully explained what the examination would involve without talking down to me. He also understood that there were questions I would not answer with him present, and he left the room to let the nurse finish them inquiry. The doctor gave me two prescriptions that I needed to take to the pharmacy. The cost was so high I could only purchase enough for 1 week. My rent was due in a few days, and I could not be late with the payment. My traditional medicines will have to do for now."

"Many of my neighbors do not have health insurance but work two and some three jobs to make ends meet. Some are documented and others are not, and I have heard stories that some have been turned away from care."

challenge assumptions about what is assumed to be normal, they are more likely to join with marginalized groups as allies to dismantle these barriers. Yolanda's experience reflects the complexity of intersectionality, positionality, and the implicit bias of the health care system (see Box 6.3).

Oppressions at the Intersections

Oppressions "intersect at innumerable points in everyday life and are mutually reinforcing, creating a total system of oppression in which one continuum of stratification cannot be addressed in isolation from all others" (Weinman, 1984, p. 169). By way of example, a Latino may have gender/sex privilege but experience ethnoracial oppression. Although a white male may experience privilege by virtue of his gender and race, he may experience oppression because of his sexual orientation, ability, nationality, and/or religion.

Oppression is entrenched in the structure of most social and economic systems, creating and maintaining human systems of violence and exploitation at all levels (Cuomo, 2003). Political, social, and economic factors cause and sustain systemic inequality. The catastrophe of Hurricane Katrina, in which over 1,800 people died, primarily from drowning, is a good example of this systemic inequality: Residents of New Orleans, Louisiana, who were marginalized by age, race, ethnicity, disabilities, and class were more likely to live in areas vulnerable to flooding, and least likely to receive either immediate assistance or the resources needed to rebuild (Cook & Rosenberg, 2015). Forty percent of those who died were age 75 or older (Cook & Rosenberg, 2015). The effects have been long lasting with many of those who left never returning (Haynes, 2015). Mechanisms such as these, which block access to resources and life opportunities, shape the lives of individuals and communities at the intersection of multiple dimensions of marginalization. Only a purposeful effort to end oppression and discrimination can reverse this system. Life in a global world requires careful self-scrutiny, as well as examination of our attitudes and beliefs, the origin of those beliefs, and the impact of those beliefs on our daily activities (Marsh, 2004). See the impact of a natural disaster on individual and family resources and privileges in Box 6.4 as a family's positional status changes in response to shifting access at the juncture of intersecting identities.

What points of intersectionality did you find? What changes occurred after the earthquake? Were privileges lost? Did oppressions remain? What impact did these factors have?

THE WEB: YESTERDAY, TODAY, AND TOMORROW

Ones position at birth can be different from one's current and future position. Although there is limited upward economic mobility in most countries, there may be changes in health/ability status, family, gender identity, economic resources, or immigrant status that can make navigating the life course more or less difficult. A person may develop a clearer understanding of their sexual orientation and/or gender identity as they age, which can disturb their own assumptions of normality. Due to war or as a result of environmental degradation, a wealthy professional with privilege in their own country may find themselves forced to live as a refugee in another country, losing most of their previous privilege based on nationality and socioeconomic status.

Create a personal Web by drawing a line to connect your positions across the wedges. Situate yourself in each section of the wheel according to your position at birth. Use a different color to situate yourself in the Web based on your current positioning. Multiple mappings can represent change or provide a representation of consistency. Examine the intersections between your various identities. Reflect on the barriers and access to resources at the intersections.

Now explore the barriers that might be created for someone who occupies multiple positions outside the central core of the Web, whether this is you or someone else. "As different forms of oppression are added to an already oppressive situation, the interactions increase exponentially, which in turn, increase the complexity of oppression on a person" (Mullaly, 2002, p. 155). An individual, family, or community experiencing ethnoracial and

Box 6.4
CHANGES FOR A HAITIAN FAMILY

On January 10, 2010, my life was forever changed. It was as if the ground would never stop shaking, buildings were crumbling, the ground opened up and swallowed everything up whole—buildings, cars, and, yes, people. It did not care if you were rich or poor, black or white, man, woman, or child. It ate them all like a monster whose hunger could not be satisfied. I can still hear the screams and cries for help, especially at night when everything was quiet. How could things that were able to stand the test of time be gone in a flash? How could my parents and maternal grandparents be gone when they promised to love me and protect me forever? My young brother and sister were upcountry visiting an auntie and cousins. It was weeks before I knew they had survived. My auntie's home was destroyed along with the roads and other important structures, but they were safe for the time being.

People were afraid to return to their homes. Some were still intact while others were reduced to rubble, so they slept on the streets. Many could not tear themselves away from where their loved ones were buried. Even the white foreigners were afraid to return to the hotels and gathered outdoors, sleeping on lawn chairs until they could be evacuated. But Haiti was our home, so we had no place to go. We waited and waited for help to come.

My name is Sophia, and I was 17 years old when the earthquake struck Haiti, where more than 100,000 people were killed and millions were left homeless. I had completed high school and was taking time off to volunteer as an aide worker before starting university. My mother said that it would be good for me to understand the needs of the people before selecting a field of study. My parents were both government workers and wanted to improve things for the Haitian people. My mother worked in public health, and my father was an engineer. I think it's important to note that my father was black, and my mother was mulatto. She came from a family of influence, which my family benefitted from. Me and my surviving brother and sister share the dark skin of our father. After months of separation I was able to reunite with my brother and sister. I was to be both mother and father and had to try to build a new life for us all.

We returned to Port-au-Prince. The university was destroyed and would not be operational for months to come. I still believed that, in time, I would be able to attend, but my current priorities were to see if any of my family's properties were still standing so that I could find a place to live. In the meantime, the United Nations aid workers had set up tents to provide temporary shelter. We heard that the United States and other foreign nations were sending aid workers and pledging millions of dollars to help with the recovery. So, if we had to stay in a tent, it would be a hardship, but we could survive because we knew that help was on the way. The most important thing for now was that my brother and sister were safe.

I mentioned earlier that my mother was mulatto and from an influential family, but her parents did not approve of the marriage and would not recognize me and my siblings as legitimate. We lost all of the important documents in the quake and subsequent fires. Therefore, I had no proof of my identity, and we all looked like our father; without the light skin of our mother. The bank would not let me access my parents' accounts, and I could not find anyone who knew my parents that would vouch for me. They were either dead or left the country. Everyone in the tent cities had to be registered, and I became number 1495—an unmarried black Haitian with two children. I feared that if I did not claim my siblings as my own, we would be separated. I could not let that happen. There were thousands of orphaned children with no place to go. The orphanages were overcrowded with few resources. We heard stories of children being sold to foreigners to relieve the overcrowding. I could not take that chance with my sister and brother.

Seven years have passed and the country seems no better off as a whole. The tent cities are still home to hundreds of thousands of people, mostly women and children, and cholera has taken many lives. Women's rights seemed to have been put on hold, and the tent cities have become breading grounds for rape and violence toward women and girls. The persistent poverty and unemployment bring out the worst in people. We do what we can to protect them, but our resources are scarce. I will continue my work for as long as I am needed.

Life has improved a bit for me, number 1495, and my siblings/children. I speak French, English, and Creole and was able to use my language skills to get a job with an aide organization. Even though I speak three languages, I still earn less than the male aid workers who only speak one. For now I do not complain. I am fortunate to be earning a salary and can take care of my siblings. We no longer live in the tent city but live in a small apartment just outside of Port-au-Prince. We all ride the tap tap, which means bus, every day to the city where the kids attend school, thanks to a mulatto patron who pays the school fees and buys their uniforms. I also continue my work in the city. I think my parents would be proud of us.

ability oppression encounters multiple barriers, including socioeconomic ones. Gender and ethnoracial identity form another intersection. Although they have historically constituted separate fields of inquiry, the concepts of race, ethnicity, and gender are so closely intertwined in individuals that it is impossible to separate the impact into separate spheres. We cannot understand gender without reference to ethnic or racial identity, nor can we consider ethnic or racial identity without considering gender (Crenshaw, 2014; White, 2001). This circles back to bell hooks's (2006, 2015) framing of white supremacy patriarchy; gender cannot be understood outside ethnoracial identity. Further, both are closely intersected with socioeconomic status. hooks (2015) explores the complex intersections across and between race, gender, and class; and the struggles of feminists to confront the barriers created at the intersections.

Context at Birth

The position (gender, country, etc.) into which we are born is one that most people in the Western world believe is not under one's control. In typical Western beliefs, there is not a choice of either our parents or our social circumstances.[1] People are believed to be thrown into a world in which the expectations of the people around us mold our roles and behavior (Young, 2000). We are each born into a context—family, culture, language, ethnoracial identity, socioeconomic status, caste, country, sex, gender, and physical and mental ability; it is generally assumed that our gender matches our sex and that we are heterosexual. We are born into a web of interactions that are strongly influenced by our social positions. We might be born into poverty; we might be born into wealth. Our caste, class, gender and sex, ethnoracial identity, nationality, sexual orientation, and ability status at birth are established. Our job is to adjust (Young, 1990).

If one is born white or lighter in skin color, there are privileges bestowed by that identity in many cultures; if one is born with darker skin color, these privileges may not be bestowed. If one is male, there are privileges; if one is presumed heterosexual, there are privileges; if one is able-bodied, there are privileges. Socioeconomic status is generally correlated with these variables, but for some, individuals with resources can mediate the impact of oppression. In each identity there is a position that is considered "the norm" or "the ideal." If one is not in this privileged group, one is seen as the "other" and is subject to the oppressions of marginalization, exploitation, powerlessness, cultural imperialism, and violence.

THE TRANSFORMATIVE IMPACT OF CRITICAL SELF-REFLECTION

The process of self-reflection and reflexivity is difficult (Marsh, 2004). Exploring the self, including one's hidden privileges and oppressions,

---

1. We recognize that some religious traditions believe we have control over the circumstances into which we are born, either because of actions in a previous life, or decisions made in between reincarnations.

opens doors for participation in critical multicultural practice. This process can be transformative and shift one's worldview. Although it is important to understand the negative impact of oppression, it is also vital to explore and appreciate the strengths and triumphs of traditionally marginalized groups. As we begin to listen to the voices of all people, we can learn from different worldviews, values, customs, family styles, and social structures. Exploration of diversity requires learning about and understanding self and others (Lum, 2010).

> When the spaces of difference are explored deeply and reflexively, then any one space may not seem so different from another. Yet . . . exploration of the spaces of difference cannot begin until we are able to hear the voices that come from those spaces. (Washington & Harris, 2001, p. 82)

This exploration of the differences and similarities within and between groups provides a base for examining individual, family, and community strengths and hardships. True learning moves beyond essentializing—seeing all people in a group as identical—and involves a critical understanding not only about the inequalities experienced by certain groups but also the intragroup diversity that reminds us of the uniqueness of each person. Each individual, each family, and each community is different. Understanding ourselves and our experiences offers the possibility for building bridges across difference (Lum, 2010).

Working in a diverse context requires an understanding of one's own assumptions, privileges, and sources of oppression and also those of the individuals and communities with whom one is working. Without this awareness, people are ill prepared to engage effectively in a global, multicultural environment. Becoming skilled in cross-cultural work recognizes and values the differences between different worldviews without negative judgment and assumptions of normality (Sue & Sue, 2016). One is able to critically evaluate and challenge the dominant cultural worldview. Self-awareness and critical reflectivity are used to examine one's own behavior and motivation and to understand the contexts within which people of different backgrounds experience their lives.

The culturally skilled professional explores the ways in which race and ethnicity, nationality, language, gender and sex, sexual orientation, income/class, and ability affect identity, educational and employment choices, and health and mental health. This work engages individuals and communities collaboratively. Through critical engagement and self-reflection it is possible to develop the skills for listening and sharing across difference. This can be translated into direct action for social change with the goal of transforming society into an equitable and just system for all community members. Collaborative engagement contributes to the dismantling of systemic structures that enforce oppressive systemic inequities.

Questions for Consideration

1. Which of your identity statuses is considered the "master status" in your country?
2. When outside your country, which identity status becomes most relevant?
3. Which identities do you hold that provide privilege? Which result in oppression?
4. How have you been affected by experiences of oppression? How have you been affected by experiences of privilege?
5. Which identities that you hold serve to mediate, mitigate, or allievate the effects of oppression?
6. What experiences have helped you develop resilience?

CHAPTER 7

Critical Multicultural Practice

Washing one's hands of the conflict between the powerful and the powerless means to side with the powerful, not to be neutral.
—Paulo Freire, *Pedagogy of the Oppressed*, 1985, p. 122

[If] we assist in making oppression acceptable by helping people to cope with it or adjust to it, we not only fail them, we fail ourselves and we become part of the problem.
—Mullaly, *Challenging Oppression: A Critical Social Work Approach*, 2002, p. 211

In this chapter we discuss critical multicultural practice with a focus on dismantling oppressive practices and structures. History is filled with calculated and sometimes brutal instances of the exclusion of people of color; women; people who are lesbian, gay, bisexual, and/or transgender (LGBT); people who are disabled; and people marginalized based on nationality, class/caste, color, or religion. Systemized racism, sexism, homophobia and heterosexism, ableism, transphobia, and classism continue to be a problem. These conditions affect communities, the lives of individuals and families, the daily practice of engaging in change, and practitioners on multiple levels. The barriers of oppression are structural—limiting access to education, employment, housing, and health care and even a clean and safe environment. Social and economic policies maintain structures that limit, or at worst, deny access; and social systems reinforce the inequality by failing to recognize or acknowledge oppressive structures and assumptions of normality. As a result, individuals, families, and communities face roadblocks that can forestall growth and create stress. Unequal access to opportunities and resources has an intergenerational impact because future generations cannot build on the resources and successes of their parents and grandparents. The goal of critical multicultural practice is to create change that involves the dismantling of systems that enforce structures of oppression at all levels.

Societal values impact the development and implementation of social and economic policies that may create structures of oppression. In a society such as Norway, traditionally, collectivism and cooperation are valued and poverty rates are low. Norwegian values support egalitarianism (Skarpenes & Sakslind, 2010), high levels of confidence and satisfaction in public/social services (Organization for Economic Cooperation and Development [OECD], 2013), and kindness toward the weak and vulnerable (van Wormer, 1994). In the United States, on the other hand, poverty rates are high, individualism and competition are valued, and individuals experiencing poverty are viewed negatively. The value base underlying policy that creates inequality can be challenged, shifting support toward a commitment to collective well-being and egalitarianism. The interplay between social and economic policy, the communities and families in which we live, the schools where we are educated, the organizations in which we work, and the media that helps frame thinking demands a multilevel response. Communities need to heal, organizations transform, and individuals and families wounded by oppressive structures require support and resources. It is also important work toward the development of policies that are socially and economically just for all.

Income inequality is a global concern. Progress has been made in reducing extreme poverty across the globe (Roser & Ortiz-Ospina, 2017). Global inequality increased rapidly over the past 200 years until recently. Although it is no longer increasing, the inequality is extremely high and will remain high for the foreseeable future (Roser & Ortiz-Ospina, 2017). Between-country inequality is higher than within-country inequality. Currently, just eight men have as much wealth as the bottom 3.6 billion people; and in the last 30 years, 7 out of every 10 people live in countries with rising inequality (OXFAM, 2016). The increasing sense of being left out economically has had negative consequences in global politics. See Box 7.1 for an exemplar from the United States of policy contributions to growing inequality. Just as with the implications globally, in the United States, policies like these contribute to growing inequality, division, and alienation.

Resistence to violence, oppression, and marginalization can take many paths. There are multiple means of resistance to oppression and multiple ways for engaging in change. However, change through collective, nonviolent action is more effective and longer lasting (Chenowith & Stephan, 2011). It assists in the development of antioppressive relationships, which can provide a base for rebuilding a political system that is nonviolent

---

Box 7.1

MANIPULATING INEQUALITY

Income inequality in the United States is at an all-time high. In 2015, the income for the top 1% was 40 times higher than that for the bottom 90%, while the income for the top 10% was 9 times more than that earned by the bottom 90%. Income for the top 1% is increasing four times faster than the bottom 20%; and currently the top 1% earn even more proportionally in after-tax dollars (192.2%) than in before-tax dollars, indicating a lower tax rate at the top. As the division grows ever wider, we must ask not only who is left out but also how and why (Income Inequality, n.d.)

Federal housing policy manipulated an increase in housing segregation and with it growth in inequality (Rothstein, 2017). The manipulated separation created a geographic divide. With limited contact, the neighborhood divide continues to widen. The increasing economic inequality grows out of and expands the divide. It is not just the top 1% that maintains this divide but the top 20%. The 19% (upper middle class, primarily white families) wield immense power over policies that favor maintaining their status and benefits (Reeves, 2017). They vote to protect benefits such as access to better education and tax benefits related to income and housing. Upper middle-class children have a different upbringing, which results in developing the attributes desired in the labor market. The related status and resources are then passed to future generations. Living with families who enjoy the same privileges and benefits, they are hidden from the impact on the other 80%.

---

and more inclusive. For instance, the women of Liberia, with the leadership of Leymah Gwobee, ended the 14-year civil war using nonviolent actions; the new government, led by a woman, is nonviolent. Circular, ongoing processes such as engaging in storytelling and restorative practices are strategies that may contribute to the necessary healing and rebuilding (Lederach & Lederach, 2010).

CRITICAL MULTICULTURAL PRACTICE WITH INDIVIDUALS AND FAMILIES

"People should be perceived not only as individuals, but also as members of social groups and cultures affected by the social, economic, and political conditions in which they live" (Kahn, 1991, p. 2). As we work with the growing diversity of an increasingly global world, this orientation becomes even more important for avoiding stereotyping and increasing our understanding of the multiple factors that impact individuals and families. Exploration of identity is key to understanding the multicultural and environmental context of individual and family functioning, group identity and membership, broad value perspectives, and sources of strength and stress. This involves learning to listen and listening to learn about how lives are shaped. It means learning about someone's view of individuals, family, and community; the significance of life events and their meaning; and learning how someone has coped with adversity and success.

Critical Assessment

A thorough critical assessment of individual, family, and community contexts engages an exploration of strengths, resources, biases, stresses, and systemic structures. Racism, classism, sexism, homophobia and heterosexism, transphobia, ableism, nativism, and other forms of discrimination and oppression are a part of our lives and therefore must be considered for their possible effects on people's lives (Lum, 2010). Assessment requires taking the time to listen and observe as a way to build relationships and gather information (see Box 7.2).

The most important lesson in this story is for service providers and other caregivers to recognize the importance of spending the time needed to listen to and respect the person who is receiving the care or services as the expert on their life. This is true for any interaction we have with another person because only the individual can know their own story. Although the worker would have learned about the family's finances once the family filled out the forms, she could never repaired the harm that was done to the helping relationship. Most important, in order to work with individuals from different cultures and backgrounds, it is essential to learn about different cultural or identity groups. Effective outcomes are dependent on an understanding of difference.

Understanding Community Context

Walters, Longres, Han, and Icard (2003) state:

> A key skill [in multicultural work] is the ability to take the role of others, that is, to see the world from the standpoint of one's clients, and from that position, to work with them and their communities to improve their lives and their social and economic conditions. (pp. 329–330)

Box 7.2

AN OLDER AFRICAN AMERICAN ADULT

My father was in the final stages of kidney disease and needed to have dialysis three times a week. The hospital worker suggested that unless a family member could take my father full time, we should consider placing him in the county nursing home. She told me not to worry or feel guilty; she knew that his children needed to work. She expressed her concern that we should not feel that we had to take on this financial hardship. In trying to develop a discharge plan for my father based on assumptions and without getting to know our family, the social worker at the hospital said she would help our family apply for welfare and medical assistance to help defray the cost of the nursing home. She also said that it would be helpful if we could obtain copies of all our financial statements in order to establish that we could not help financially. If we were proactive and got all the paperwork together, she could establish that we were not able to help. She wanted my dad to receive all the benefits that he was entitled to. She stated that everything would be "smooth sailing" since she was "100% certain" that dad was eligible for many of the social programs and nursing home placement based on need.

She felt my father may also have early signs of dementia since he did not seem to be lucid at times. I was surprised to hear this, since neither the doctor nor I had noticed any signs of this. Reluctantly, I asked her how she came to this conclusion. She responded slowly, allowing me time to comprehend. She reported that he was unable to recall information regarding his life. She went on to say that when she interviewed my father and asked him some questions about his life, he rambled. I asked her to be patient with me and reconstruct her conversation with my dad, as that would help me to understand.

She smiled when she said my father reminded her of an old African American family friend whom she called "Pops." Pops was employed by her parents to maintain the gardens and fix things at her home. She saw my father as a cute elderly African American man and felt it was okay to call my dad "Pops." I grimaced but did not let her see it. In our family we were taught to call anyone older than us "Mister" or "Missus." I wondered why this worker felt free to call my dad "Pops."

She said that my father said he was married and that he attended and graduated from the Mecca. He talked about Jack and Jill, the Links, and the Ques. He also told her he was a knight. He told her that he was ready for his homecoming but had hoped that he could stay in his own home until it was his time. At that point, she said he was not making much sense. She said she asked him a few follow-up questions to get the information she needed, but he seemed to get frustrated and agitated, so she decided to end the interview.

I knew exactly what the problem was as soon as she gave me this information. Do you? Let's review just a few of the critical issues and assumptions that she failed to explore.

First, the worker did not follow the golden rule: She did not use the strengths perspective, and she failed to explore our social, familial, and economic resources and history. Her intention was to work in the client's best interest, but her ability to do this was obstructed by the stereotypes she held about people of color and older adults. She never asked the father or the family if financial assistance was needed. She assumed that they were emotionally supportive but did not have the time or the funds to assist their father. She failed to talk with all parties about how the father and the family felt about alternate placements or aging in place (staying in his own home).

Several assumptions were made that narrowed the scope of the assessment. Remember that the worker stated that this gentleman reminded her of someone from her past. She somehow determined that this man was of the lower socioeconomic status, perhaps just like the family friend named Pops. She even felt that she had the right (white privilege behavior) to call him by this other man's name. In essence, the worker failed to ask what help the family wanted, what resources were available, or how she should address the father.

Third, she went so far as to state that she felt the father was experiencing dementia. She assumed that information that did not make sense to her was a sign of dementia. She misunderstood words and phrases related to his African American experience. Had she used her lack of knowledge as a base to engage the family in discussion, she would have learned what the terms used by the father meant. Although no one person can know everything about another culture or identity, the worker failed to ask others if the father's "babble" meant something to them. Unfortunately, the worker just assumed this was a symptom of dementia, which caused her client and his family great frustration. When the client referred to the Mecca, he was referring to Howard University, a historically black institution in Washington, D.C.; Jack and Jill and the Links are social organizations that African American families join to develop a strengths perspective about African American history, culture, and socialization opportunities. Both of these organizations provide numerous networks for members. Many middle- and upper-class African Americans are members of Jack and Jill and Links. When the father referred to himself as a Que, this meant that he was a member of Omega Psi Phi, a national African American fraternity for men. When he said he was a knight, he was referring to yet another organization, the Knights of Columbus, which is a Catholic fraternal (benefit) organization. Many African Americans use the word "homecoming" as a euphemism to refer to one's time to die and go to heaven.

Had the worker listened without making assumptions, she would have had a base of questions for gathering information. As she filled in the gaps, she would have learned that the father attended and graduated from a university. She would also have learned that his social circle was vast, since he was affiliated with numerous social organizations. The father could have enough caring people in his social network to age in place. Finally, and most important, she would have explored whether or not the father and his children had a financial plan that would allow them to provide the resources he needed.

Social constructionist theory supports this model of practice by framing analysis around how individuals and communities make sense of the activities and events in their world. The interchange between people and their environmental, cultural, and historical contexts is emphasized by social constructionist theory. Understanding this interchange between a person and their environment, and the meanings they attach to that interchange, is critical to a meaningful assessment (Mallon, 1999b). The strengths-based and narrative models of practice build from the social constructionist theory and enable this process. Adding this complexity does not mean permitting a chaotic mess; rather, it involves an analysis that is deep, nuanced, and textured, and that can be articulated in a way that all can understand. When our models and metaphors betray us, we need to develop new models. Of course, recall the adage that the only thing more difficult than getting a new idea in, is getting an old idea out.

Culture, identity, class, caste, resources, nationality, and social context are critical elements that shape struggles and affect an individual's ability to develop coping resources (Devore & Schlesinger, 1998). These interactions influence the development of individual, family, and community worldviews (Lum, 2010). Family and community impact the potential income, education, and lifestyle of an individual. The interchange is a complex one in which strengths frequently intermingle with fears and vulnerabilities. Situational interchanges, historical and cultural influences, and the interpretation of experiences affect the construction of meaning, vision, and perception.

Individuals, families, and communities do not exist in a vacuum or in isolation. Within each is a complex intersection of ethnoracial identity, gender and sex, gender identity, nationality, class, caste, and sexual orientation as well as ability, economic resources, history, language, political system, and religion. Just practice requires the worker to acknowledge and understand "the intersection and complex interaction of multiple social identities and a continuum of harm and privilege that confer these identities" (Van Soest, 2003, p. 345).

Critical assessment and practice involve building knowledge regarding historical and social policy views, ecological as well as ethnoracial and class contexts, and feminist and other antioppression perspectives. Ecological assessment sets the stage for informed response, providing an outline for evaluation of the dimensions of personal and structural oppression. Through antioppressive practice, people individually and collectively are engaged in tasks that help them remediate the damage created by oppression while also creating solidarity by building community (Mullaly, 2002, 2010). The triumph experienced in the social change process builds strength.

Leigh's (1998) ethnographic interview is one tool that can be used to guide this process. The ethnographic interview involves an interactive process of learning about the individual within their context. The process of building rapport opens a window to the individual and collective worldviews and cultural interpretation of events. It begins with a global exploration of culture and history. Personal and family history, multilevel resilience factors, and experiences of abuse and trauma are evaluated. Individual, family, and community strengths and resources are assessed.

People who are members of communities that are historically marginalized are affected by societal and professional attitudes, biases, and actions. For example, transgender individuals may be coping with feelings of guilt, shame, fear, anxiety, low self-esteem, anger, and isolation as a result of societal intolerance. They bring with them family history (positive and negative), personal trauma, interactions within social networks, and a possible history of adjustment issues. Comfort with and knowledge of the issues faced by transgender individuals are significant determinants of the quality of the interaction. The issues are more complex for transgender people at the intersection of race; people of color who are transgender experience a unique and more intense oppression (Gainor, 2000).

Because people exist within environments, healing is contextual. Critical multicultural practice must be based on an ongoing dialogue about the strengths and resources that can support the person, family, and community. Interventions that build from systems theory, emphasize the social environment, and embrace the strengths perspective often are a better fit for populations that are marginalized (see Lum, 2010). In recognizing the similarities and differences, one values the uniqueness of each human being. "Certainly, this attitude and approach to people as particular persons is the beginning of cultural competence" (Lum, 2010, p. 34).

Narrative and Story

The narrative model emerges from the constructionist paradigm supporting interventions that are forward moving and hopeful. Stories and storytelling are methods for creating, sustaining, and transmitting meaning (Holland & Kilpatrick, 1993). Because meaning is socially constructed through exchange and interchange, storying provides a venue for facilitating change. The collaborative exploration of stories offers individuals, families, and communities the possibility to restory, reframe, and reorganize the narrative so that it becomes restorative. As Saleebey (1994) notes, "Meaning, whether manifested in story, narrative, vision, or language, affects intention and action, feeling and mood, relationships, interactions with the surrounding world, well-being, and possibility" (p. 355).

In narrative practice, life stories are shared in interactional engagement (Lum, 2010). Narrative and storytelling emphasize strengths, providing the base for a positive approach to practice (Saleebey, 1994). Adversity can leave people (individually and collectively) with conflicting feelings of guilt, shame, and anger. Supporting the building of more empowering memories of negative events facilitates the process of growth. Recalling memories of successful coping encompasses embracing the totality of experience, not just the pain. The highlighting of positive experiences, supportive relationships, and interactions places a focus on resilience, healing, and the potential for transformative change. Considering the conditions confronting past generations helps with understanding social structures and individual choice (Senehi et al., 2009).

For instance, through restorying, lesbian, gay, and bisexual individuals, as well as their families, can build self-esteem, an internal sense of worth and value, and a vision of a future with positive possibilities. Working with lesbians and gay men involves learning the impact of homophobia and heterosexism. Coming-out stories can be a means of sharing one's challenges and successes in openly identifying as a member of an oppressed population. Collections of coming-out stories in social media also allow one to see changes across generations of LGBT people. Narrative and storytelling may also empower lesbians and gay men of color who are often caught between four communities (the gay or lesbian community, the ethnoracial community, one's gender group, and the community of gay or lesbian people of color) to act as a cultural bridge (Walters et al., 2003).

Reflection on the stories told by people, groups, and communities allows exploration and understanding of diverse life experiences (Holland & Kilpatrick, 1993). These stories can also build bridges to connect communities, and therefore the use of stories supports multicultural engagement (Holland & Kilpatrick, 1993). Narrative practice occurs through the exploration of individual and collective stories engaging cultural myths, rituals, and concerns from which people, families, and communities construct meaning. Centering cultural values can help with guiding people through difficult experiences toward the path to social justice (Senehi et al., 2009).

Storytelling can be used constructively to give voice to intergroup conflict and motivate action/change (Senehi, 2002). Storytelling can encompass the complexity of intergroup conflicts recognizing divisions and facilitate the building of cross-group and interpersonal understanding (Senehi, 2002). The individual is the creator of the story that is told. In working in community, we can facilitate the telling of a story that guides movement toward social justice.

Strengths, Empowerment, and Resilience

The strengths-based model is recognized as appropriate practice with individuals, families, and communities that have experienced oppression and marginalization (Devore & Schlesinger, 1998). It is a model that provides an opportunity to view individuals, situations, and environments from a perspective of possibility and resilience (Saleebey, 2002). The impact of adversity is heavily influenced by a person's resilience. Multiple factors in the individual, family, and community support the development of resilience. Facing adversity, recognizing the potential for growth, building self-esteem, and viewing the self as capable create resilience. Resilience, in turn, provides support and strength in times of stress. This knowledge is critical in work with marginalized populations. Stories offer opportunities to find personal and interpersonal strengths that form the framework for resilience (see Box 7.3).

Where is the resilience in Layla's story that we can use to help her with transitioning? What forms of violence and oppression are present? What factors in her life supported her in facing adversity? What identities interact that both increase resilience and vulnerability? What new intersections is Layla now facing?

Cultural connections and positive racial pride are also dimensions of resilience (Lafromboise, Coleman, & Gerton, 1993; Miller & MacIntosh, 1999). In indigenous communities, positive cultural identification and participation in traditional events buffer the impact of adversity (Waller & Yellow Bird, 2002). Similarly, positive identity development in lesbians and gay men of color can buffer the stresses of heterosexism and homophobia,

Box 7.3
SYRIAN REFUGEE: RESILIENCE AMONG ADVERSITY

Layla, a 17-year-old Syrian Muslim woman, recently arrived in a major city in Sweden through the refugee resettlement program. She arrived alone without family or friends. This is her story. Because of the violence in Syria and gender oppression at home and while trying to migrate to safety, Layla's intersecting positionality has shifted for her and her mother. Their vulnerability has increased as they consciously work to decrease Layla's vulnerability through education.

My mother and I left our home and all of our possessions when the fighting and violence took the lives of my father and two uncles. I was 15 at the time and my mother was being pressured to marry me off to a much older uncle so that he would provide protection for me and my mother. I had dreams of finishing school and becoming a doctor; my mother wanted these outcomes for me as well. After much prayer and discussion, we made the most agonizing decision to leave. We sold everything we could to have enough money to escape. We had to pay men to smuggle us out. Everything cost too much money, but we had little choice.

We stayed in refugee camps in Turkey and Jordan for a few months each. The conditions there were difficult. It is particularly difficult for women traveling without a father, uncle, or older brother. My mother and I were often propositioned with offers of sex for food, sex for water, sex for information. We at times went hungry because we would not comply. My mother would remind me that we were strong women and we could endure. We were able to get to Lebanon and Iraq and stayed in small cramped apartments with many other people. The women who were traveling alone were often forced to share sleeping areas with strange men. My mother and I would take turns sleeping to keep a lookout. Sometimes we moved several times in short succession. We would go days without bathing, and when we did, the men would watch. We would take turns holding up a blanket for a little privacy. I could tell that my mother was losing strength, but she would not complain. We thought it would take about 3 months to find our way to the United States, but after 9 months we were still waiting. I had missed almost a year of school and was homesick for my family and friends.

Sleeping at night was difficult not just because I missed my home and school but I have seen things that haunt me, particularly the deaths of people in my community. I did not see my father die, but I did see my uncle beaten, shot, and dragged through the streets. There are things I cannot speak of that happened to women and girls; I've said too much already. I miss my mother, but, when I was offered asylum in Sweden, she was too ill to be granted the papers to join me. She made me promise to continue the journey and fulfill my dream of becoming a doctor. I won't disappoint her.

sexism, and racism (Walters et al., 2003). Identifying resilience and survival strategies in individuals, families, and communities of reference facilitates the development of coping strategies and supports growth.

Strengths-based practice is focused on exploring opportunities, capacities, and possibilities (Mackelprang & Salsgiver, 1999). It is an affirming model that fosters discovery and growth. At the local or individual level people are engaged in the exploration and reinforcement of strengths with the goal of developing and realizing dreams (Saleebey, 2002). For instance, models of strength combined with supportive environments are vital in work with transgender children and youth (Mallon, 1999b). When working with persons with disabilities, encouraging involvement in community and policy change may empower individuals and communities (Mackelprang & Salsgiver, 1999). Individual strengths are nurtured, while environmental resources and community responsiveness are increased. These lessons are significant for work with marginalized and stigmatized communities.

Restorative Practices

The United Nations recognizes restorative practices as a way to repair harm (Reimer et al., 2015). These are healing practices that bring together all affected parties at the individual, community, and national levels. Empowerment is integral to restorative practices (Mallon, 1999c). Through restorative practices and processes, individuals, families, and communities that previously saw themselves in conflict are supported as they engage in collaborative healing and change. Assessment and change require knowledge about personal and systemic/structural issues. In restorative practice, stories are retold from a position of strength and resistance, rather than from a position of isolation and assimilation (Walters et al., 2003).

At a mega level, as systems move away from conflict, they need to heal and rebuild community. This is a long-term and ongoing process that involves healing, forgiveness, and reconciliation. Rwanda provides a case study that highlights the complexity of the healing process (see Outreach Program on the Rwanda Genicide and the United Nations, 2012). The truth and reconciliation process can occur at the local and national levels. It is an ongoing process. Without the ongoing process of healing, forgiveness, and reconciliation, conflict often returns. Reimer (2014) describes the process of colonization in Canada, the long-standing oppression of indigenous communities, and the process of restorative healing that the government has started to engage. This includes an apology and reparations for the abuses indigenous peoples have suffered and continue to suffer.

The use of restorative practices within justice systems focuses on healing for all parties involved, including the offenders. In restorative practices, it is important to support the offenders and victims/targets, maintaining their humanity and connection to the community (Chen, Duliani, & Piepzna-Samarasinha, 2011). The retributive criminal justice system, on the other hand, focuses on blame and punishment; the state brings charges against the offender. Within the retributive system the victim and other community members are often harmed or disregarded (Reimer et al., 2015). As we struggle to find ways to support our most marginalized communities, we must consider alternative models of justice that do not revictimize survivors or further add to the oppression and injustice experienced in our communities.

New Zealand has progressive restorative practice models that incorporate Maori indigenous community-building methods. Some models involve the restorying and re-engaging of youth in indigenous cultures. In New Zealand's Family Group Conferences model, the offender hears directly from people harmed about the traumatic impact of the offender's behavior on other persons (MacRae & Zehr, 2004). These models have spread globally and hold out hope for justice for marginalized communities seeking to address injustice.

MOBILIZING FOR CHANGE

Critical multiculturalism is a theoretical and ideological stance that is compatible with the practice and values of professionals working in communities. It is a concept that embraces diversity and justice and seeks to dismantle oppression (Schmitz, Stakeman, & Sisneros, 2001). The antioppression focus encourages the use of practice models that strive for a more inclusive future. Through critical multicultural practice, the potential exists to participate in systemic change (Giroux, 1997). The complexity of the issues facing people and the complexity of the context require learning across cultures and engaging change at individual through global levels simultaneously. Critical pedagogy is key to creating a context for change within the context of globalization and authoritarian politics (Giroux, 2011).

Too often, the voices that have advocated change have been silenced. The code of silence within professional and educational organizations keeps professionals from exposing structural, cultural, and direct violence, which most often affects women, people of color, low-income people, people of different sexual orientations and gender identities, people who are disabled, and immigrants, refugees, and asylum seekers. Classrooms and organizational and community spaces can and should become what McLaren (1997) calls "spaces of hope" that support individual and societal transformation. These spaces of hope and the transformative feelings they engender are not only individual and psychological but also structural and political.

The historical narrative is written in the voice of those with privilege, and policy is often created through the explicit and implicit bias of the policy makers who cannot recognize and cannot acknowledge their privilege. Too often the voices of people who are marginalized (and their allies) become invisible as they are excluded from the historical record. Validating the strengths and resilience, along with the sources, history, and hidden nature of structural and systemic oppression, is necessary to critical education. Owning histories of bias (explicit and implicit) and oppression is a beginning point.

Our historical narrative has to be inclusive of people who are marginalized and people who are privileged. To be otherwise denies the resilience, knowledge, and strengths of those who have been marginalized structurally while negating the responsibility of those with privilege for being active learners and workers in the change process. Without the inclusion of everyone in examining history, the possibilities for building bridges toward transformative change are limited. Those who write or control the dominant discourse in a society often silence or overlook voices that acknowledge the strengths, resilience, and innovation of marginalized peoples. Too often, we are distracted from the possibilities for resilience in the face of oppression.

Community dialogues can create spaces for rehumanizing groups who share space and face similar struggles. Discussions that are issue based rather than divided along political lines do not take away the tension and fear, but they can create spaces where the possiblity exists to lower the tension, opening the potential for learning to listen (see Stone, Patton, & Heen, 2010). "Dialogue is a process for talking about tension-filled topics. It is useful for families, small groups, businesses, communities, organizations, and national and international conflicts" (Schirch & Campt, 2007, p. 5). Communities are using the dialogue process for a broad range of goals, including planning, development, ending violence, and engaging a sharing of identity conflicts. Dialogues are guided processes with a focus on enhancing communication with a goal toward building relationships and community. A major aim is to create a space for civil and respectful listening; they require a commitment to learning from people who might have very different beliefs (see Schirch & Kampt, 2007, for a full overview of the process).

The potential for change is often found in the common need for the development, access to, and control of local resources. Often the common passion comes back to resources for children, respect across identity, or ability to meet daily needs. Saving the children was the motivating factor for the women of Liberia. Through interconnection and the development of mutual respect, communities can cultivate collaborations that build capacity for identifying ways to fight for rebuilding, identifying, and further developing local resources. The commitment to valuing unique cultures and identities is the backbone for building civic space (Maalouf, 2012). The dismantling of borders within communities and across rural and urban communities can create webs of change.

Caring, compassion, and spiritual commitment produce powerful emotions to motivate change. Community is about belonging; it is about decreasing isolation (Block, 2009; hooks, 2009). A renewed sense of hope is engendered as collective action engages social and political process through advocacy, organizing, and community building. Organizing creates an environment in which individuals and communities can learn to share power and work toward empowerment (Kahn, 1991). Although this can be challenging, it can also lead to the development of comradeship and collective empowerment as social justice values are translated into practice.

It has long been recognized that collective action can disrupt the negative impact of oppressive social and economic policies confronting marginalized communities (Kahn, 1991). This process offers the potential for growth by providing an opportunity for people to find their voice, develop collectivity, acquire skills, and create hope. As individuals work together toward community change, individual and relational dynamics are restructured. Individuals are empowered as they advocate change. In the process, worldviews, relationship patterns, and personal potential are altered. Change often creates conflicts, which have the potential for precipitating transformative change. The change can start at the government level, at the community level, and/ or the local level, which can be the most effective.

Creating and rebuilding community is essential for bringing individuals and families out of isolation and into belonging (Block, 2009; hooks, 2009). Change comes in moving beyond individual "change" to community transformation through connection, relationship, and mutual empathy. "Communitiy offers the promise of belonging and calls for us to acknowledge our interdependence" (Block, 2009, p. 3). Allies—people who are supportive of the disenfranchised group—play an important role, expanding those invested in the process of change (Ayvazian, 2001). Communities can serve as sites for the development necessary to minimize and adapt to global issues such as climate change (McMichael, 2017).

Nonviolent change movements are long lasting and more effective (Chenowith & Stephan, 2011). They are also flexible and broad ranging in potential methods for responding quickly to changes in the context and risk level (see Sharp, 1973, for additional information on methods of non-violent action).

Organizational Leadership

Organizations help structure and support transformative change. Spaces designed to be inclusive of diversity tend to display an overall welcoming environment. These organizations are also likely to exhibit a commitment to advocacy and community change. Culturally effective practice can occur in all activities and at all organizational levels (McPhatter & Ganaway, 2003). Key leaders within organizations set the tone; their support is crucial to engaging critical multicultural practice. The process of transformation is supported through structural and environmental change, along with training and knowledge building.

Culturally responsive leadership is key to critical multicultural practice. A collaborative reflective process helps with the recognition of cultural positions and biases, and supports collective learning through storytelling (Abt-Perkins, Hauschildt, & Dale, 2000). Through this process, individuals and systems can reflect on their fears, silences, and areas where they lack knowledge and awareness.

Leadership is about listening and facilitating. Leaders enable the building of hope and transformation in organizations and communities. True leaders are humble (Collins, 2001). They focus on developing inclusive structures, spaces, and attitudes. Transformational leaders inspire, model, challenge, enable, and encourage (Kouzes & Posner, 2017). They do not force their vision and structure; they do not see themselves as being at the center or the most important. A knowledge of organizational dynamics and a multisystem process guides organizational transformation (Mallon, 1999a; McPhatter, 1997).

WICKED PROBLEMS

"Wicked problems" are issues that are complicated, multilayered, and difficult to solve yet are so significant that we have to try (Conklin, 2006).

Although there is no single list, social injustice, violent conflict, extreme poverty, increasing economic inequality, global migration, environmental degradation, and climate change meet the criteria for wicked problems. To add to the complexity, each wicked problem is a symptom of another problem. These problems are intertwined (World Commission, 1987) and so is the potential for transformative change. Although the complex interdependencies make it impossible to solve the problems, the opportunity for transformation exists within the complexity. Interdisciplinary practice and research engages new analytic lenses, creating the potential for meaningful change. These concerns require thoughtful reflection that challenge disciplinary boundaries and urge participants to explore alternative models for engaging change (Schmitz, Matyók, James, & Sloan, 2013).

Although it might be considered the responsibility of the government to promote the well-being of all citizens, responses to these problems are increasingly inadequate as the expansion of wealth continues to grow more concentrated among the few (Income Inequality, n.d.; Kahn, 1991). These divisions and perception of difference have been used to demonize and exclude people considered as "the other." With political and ideological conflict, governments run by those with privilege use separation of the other to justify oppression and inequality. In the United States, black men and boys are considered the other. Due to explicit and implicit bias, this fact and the high risk black men and boys face are too often overlooked and even denied. This is true even when they are unjustly killed. Moore, Adedoyin, and Robinson (2017) documented the police brutality, including the murder of black males who were unarmed. The polarization continues to grow with the militarization of police and the increasing fear of the police in the community.

Too often the discussion about inequality and injustice is refocused away from these problems and becomes a way to blame and create fear that divides communities. This distracts community members from finding commonalities in their fight for justice. The politics of hate creates borders within communities that result in the silencing of marginalized voices. As the voices of populations within communities are divided, the larger community loses the potential for the collective action needed to combat structural oppression, injustice, inequality, and environmental issues that threaten their very health.

Following is an exploration of overlapping wicked problem: refugees, global migration, the justice system, climate change, environmental justice, and sustainability. At the end, there are questions for the reader to consider in identifying how the application of critical multicultural practice could be used to begin to address these global crises.

Refugees and Global Migration

As of 2017, there are more people displaced/pushed from their home (65.6 million people) than previously recorded; a third (22.5 million) of those are refugees. Half of those refugees are under 18 years of age (United Nations High Commission on Refugees [UNHCR], 2017). The UNHCR provides supplies and protections at refugee camps across more than 125 countries with 1.9 million housed in the 50 largest camps (Esri, 2013). Many of these camps are not temporary; they are the only homes some of the younger refugees have known.

Refugees flee because of adverse conditions at home. Too often they are leaving communities/countries engaged in brutal violent conflict or facing the starvation that results from ongoing conflict and/or climate change. The plight of refugees is also one of risk (see Amena's story in Box 7.4).

As experienced by Amena, the journey of a refugee is often lengthy and filled with peril, particularly for women and children/youth. The losses of home, nation, friends, family, and sense of security compound the impact. Education, health care, and employment are difficult to access.

Working with refugees and immigrants means recognizing the multi-layered loss of friends, family, language, home, and general comfort experienced by refugees and other immigrants. It also means identifying and building from individual, family, and community strengths. The transitions experienced by refugees require negotiating new surroundings with unfamiliar sights and sounds, interactional patterns, social relationships, structural forces, and language patterns. Models link resilience to strengths, temperament, and environment (Hutchinson, Stuart, & Pretorius, 2010), offering clues to the significance of characteristics and resources for building strengths and resilience. Studies support the significance of social connection in creating and strengthening community resilience (Ellis & Abdi, 2017).

Connecting with our own or others' stories of strength and resilience in the face of social upheaval, war, and trauma can be an antidote to what might otherwise be the internalization of a sense of powerlessness, depression, fear, or even shame. (Senehi et al., 2009, n.p.)

Connecting with others and their stories becomes more important with the global rise in nationalism, which is increasing isolation. The accompanying anti-immigrant feelings create a negative environment that needs to be considered when working with refugees, asylum seekers, and other immigrants. Families from immigrant and refugee communities entering

---

Box 7.4

AMENA: THE RISK FOR REFUGEES

Amena is one of millions of South Sudanese asylum seekers to have fled her home because of the violent conflict and the resulting starvation in the South Sudan. Her father was killed in one of the raids, and she witnessed the deaths of many others. Because of the war, her family went hungry for days at a time. After months of fear that they would die of starvation, in 2015 Amena and her family left in search of food and safety from the violence. She joined a million other refugees from South Sudan in Uganda at one of the four refugee centers.

At the refugee camp, conditions were difficult for Amena and her family. Access to food and shelter was limited. She survived on the meager humanitarian aid available in the camp. Her diet was poor with no fruits or vegetables for the year she was in the camp. She did not attend school. Like other girls, she often faced abuse and struggled to avoid a forced marriage.

A year later, Amena's mother was able to get her smuggled into Germany, where she moved to an arrival center for processing as an orphan. Conditions in the arrival center were not much better than the refugee camp in Uganda, and she was still not able to attend school. After 3 months, she was moved to an orphanage in Munich, where she shares a room with 10 other girls. Although she was hoping to return to school, the orphanage has only a couple of volunteer teachers. She occasionally gets to take a class in German. Many of the children who arrived at the orphanage left because the formal processes of reconnecting them with relatives in other countries was lengthy, or because there were inadequate supervision and resources for the children. Amena remains, hoping to go to school and be reunited with her family one day.

---

new lives are at risk of traumatic adjustment. This involves negotiating new surroundings with unfamiliar sights and sounds, interactional patterns, social relationships, structural forces, and language patterns.

For refugees, transitions are often compounded by a history of terror and multiple displacements (Devore & Schlesinger, 1998; Schmitz et al., 2003). The loss is exacerbated further for women and girls, particularly those of color (Lie & Lowery, 2003). Refugee women have the "added burdens of issues emanating from the horrors of war, forced migration, and relocation" (Lie & Lowery, 2003, p. 299). Resilience can build from social healing when communities are faced with sustained violence (Lederach & Lederach, 2010). "It is incumbent upon professionals committed to social and economic justice, to comprehensively understand the range of obstacles facing immigrants and refugees and empower them in their struggle to make a healthy adjustment" (Schmitz et al., 2003, p. 135).

Climate Change, Environmental Justice, and Sustainability

Climate change and environmental degradation fuse together as a wicked problem linked to many others, including global migration, violent conflict, and poverty. These issues are at the root of changes in local and global communities that exacerbate growing inequality and an increase in the "othering" of vulnerable populations, disproportionally impacting marginalized communities. Ecological degradation is a complex, multifaceted problem with multiple tentacles easily exploited to create confusion and division. Climate change and environmental degradation are closely linked to the refugee crisis. Climate change and conflicts over the exhausted resources multiply the threat (Intergovernmental Panel on Climate Change [IPCC], 2015). Forecasts for environmental migrants are highly variable, ranging from 25 million to 1 billion "with 200 million being the most widely cited estimate" (International Organization for Migration [IOM], n.d.; IPCC, 2015).

The World Commission on Environment and Development recognizes the interconnection across peace, security, development, and environmental sustainability (World Commission, 1987). War and extreme economic inequality are linked to structural violence in the human community and to the degradation of the biophysical environment. Misuse of natural resources, natural disasters, and climate change do not respect borders and can only be addressed by creating links locally and then more globally. Government policies impact people directly and indirectly, privileging some while challenging others.

Wangari Maathai (see Box 7.5) was a leader of change that encompassed overlapping wicked problems. What began as ecological morphed across community, violence, gender oppression, and structural/political change. Wangari Maathai moved from the micro to the mega, building relationships and community. She did not back down to power, nor was she alone as a nonviolent community movement emerged. The movement continued to grow and expand into a community education and development program where people learned the responsibilities of citizenship. They created government change and engaged the army in the change process. She became a global leader.

Box 7.5

WANGARI MAATHAI: LEADING CHANGE

Wangari Maathai was a globally educated Kenyan citizen, a community-level activist and organizer, and a change agent at local and global levels. Educated first in her local community, she knew the value of the earth and the life that depends on ecological health. She received a scholarship to study biology in the United States, receiving her baccalaureate and master's degrees in biology. After returning to Kenya, she completed her PhD, becoming the first woman in East Africa to earn a doctorate. In the process, she found her voice as an activist and change agent.

She began her career as an activist by engaging the women of the community in germinating and planting trees (Merton & Dater, 2008). Because she was a woman, those in power did not see the power of her organizing early in the process. This project resulted in rebuilding the ecological environment and the community as the women were empowered. She went on to found The Green Belt Movement (The Green Belt Movement, n.d.), and in 2004 she was the first woman in Africa to be awarded the Nobel Peace Prize for the contributions she made to sustainability, democracy, and peace. She resisted government oppression as an actor in and out of the government. She stated, "Human rights are not things that are put on the table for people to enjoy. These are things you fight for and then you protect" (Maathai, n.d.).

Being a highly educated woman in Kenya did not come without its challenges. Kenya, like most countries, is a patriarchal society in which men hold the power, dominate in politics, and control property. Within the family, fathers or father figures hold authority over women and children. Maathia was attempting to do what no other woman in Kenya had done before her. As an activist, she led the process of women's empowerment; at this point, she became a threat to the government. She and her colleagues were threatened, arrested, beaten, and violently intimidated. Global allies with power pressured the government in ways that helped safeguard Wangari Maathai and her colleagues.

The Green Belt Movement successfully recruited local women to grow tree seedlings to plant in their communities. As a result of the seedlings successfully taking root and growing, the land erosion decreased and drinking water was cleaner. The women were paid a small stipend for every seedling that matured. The project went beyond planting trees, with the local women being encouraged to invest their earnings in creating small businesses. Some groups of women bought bees to cultivate honey to be sold at the local markets; some purchased goats to breed and for the sale of milk. As their earnings grew, they reinvested their monies to expand their businesses. Earning an income meant that they would be able to pay school fees to send their daughters and sons to school, and purchase food and medicines when needed. Traditionally, if there was only enough money to send one child to school, the girls were often the second choice. The Green Belt Project created hope and a future that went well beyond the forests. It has given future generations the knowledge that the environment matters and they have a role in caring for and protecting it. "When people are hungry and have food for only today, they do not think about what will happen when they cut down the last tree. They only realize the damage when it's too late" (Strides in Development, 2010).

Wangari Maathia (2003) and bell hooks (2009) developed models for change based on understanding the value of education and connection to the land. As a town or neighborhood comes together to address climate change or environmental degradation, they build relationships, engage in political knowledge building, build community, and empower themselves. Education, outreach, and dialogue are needed to support the process of change and create links across identity groups.

As ecological degradation occurs, it disproportionately affects groups of people who can be understood as disenfranchised, marginalized, and oppressed—this has a profound impact globally on human rights and social justice concerns (Besthorn, 2013; Bullard, 1994; Coates, 2003, 2005; Zapf, 2009). The entire ecology is impacted with the loss of flora and fauna. Creating change includes eliminating the production and use of toxins that contaminate soil, air, and water, which contributes to insufficient and/or unsafe access to food and water for humans and nonhumans alike. The result is polluted water, brownfields, and increased asthma rates often in the poorest neighborhoods, requiring corrective responses that address restoring health for individuals and communities. Ultimately, climate change is a significant factor precipitating deteriorating political and economic systems, forcing increased international migration. The crisis is global in nature, requiring a holistic response.

CONCLUSION

I'm very conscious of the fact that you can't do it alone. It's teamwork. When you do it alone you run the risk that when you are no longer there nobody else will do it.
—Wangari Maathai, *The Green Belt Movement*, 2003, p. 138

The quest for social, economic, and environmental justice is supported by practice models that are based on critical pedagogy and that engage the theory of social construction (Devore & Schlesinger, 1998). A multifaceted focus on the individual, the ecological environment, and issues of social and economic justice strengthens marginalized communities (Appleby, Colon, & Hamilton, 2001). Personal narratives can become a tool for supporting the development of the transforming skills (Tully, 2000). This is a visioning approach that incorporates individual, community, and neighborhood resources and strengths (Mackelprang & Salsgiver, 1999). The provision of advocacy and the alleviation of isolation and depression through community action empower individuals and communities.

Communities and nations are facing problems of increasing magnitude and complexity, including growing inequality, war, political unrest, global migration, and climate change/environmental degradation. These are not problems that can be changed through two-dimensional models and the efforts of one discipline. At all levels and across multiple systems, helping professionals are obligated to identify human rights concerns, social inequities, instances of oppression, ecological violence, and other forms of injustice. In exceptional times providers who are members of professions with a strong value base can serve as a guiding anchor (Snyder, 2017). As Snyder states, "If members of a profession think of themselves as groups with common interests, norms and rules that oblige them at all times, they can gain confidence and indeed a certain kind of power" (p. 40). If in our personal and professional lives, "we assist in making oppression acceptable by helping people to cope with it or adjust to it, we not only fail them, we fail ourselves and we become part of the problem" (Mullaly, 2002, p. 211).

Critical multicultural practice in an era of "wicked" problems requires engaging complexity and creativity. Charged with serving marginalized populations means addressing systemic inequality. To achieve justice as the world grows smaller through the process of globalization, there need to be changes in the commitment of resources to support education, health care, retraining, and social security systems (Friedman, 2006). Answers do not come easily; and change often has its roots in the building of bridges through dialogue, education, outreach, and relationship building. Professions shaped by a strong value base can be leaders in the change process.

Questions for Consideration

1. What are the structures and systems that limit access for marginalized communities? How are these rationalized? How do cultural beliefs and value structures serve to maintain these systems?

2. How are the misuse of power, inequality, and marginal access to resources rationalized? Who benefits from these dynamics?
3. How does income inequality look in your community or country?
4. What policies and practices are used to maintain poverty and income inequality in your country?
5. In what ways are your community and your country impacted by environmental degradation?
6. How can we transform social structures? What resources do you think should be made available?
7. How can you serve as an ally?

REFERENCES

Aboriginal Heritage Office. (2017). *A brief aboriginal history*. Retrieved from http://www.aboriginalheritage.org/history/history

Abt-Perkins, D., Hauschildt, P., & Dale, H. (2000). Becoming multicultural supervisors: Lessons from a collaborative field study. *Journal of Curriculum and Supervision, 16*(1), 28–47.

Ackah, W. (1999). *Pan–Africanism: Exploring the contradictions: Politics, identity and development in Africa and the African diaspora*. New York, NY: Routledge.

Act No. 30 of 1950. (n.d.). [An act to register the population of the union]. Retrieved from http://www.sahistory.org.za/sites/default/files/DC/leg19500707.028.020.030/leg19500707.028.020.030.pdf

Adichie, C. N. (2014). *We should all be feminists*. New York, NY: Anchor Books.

Africa Policy Information Center. (1997). *Talking about tribe: Moving from stereotype to analysis*. Retrieved from http://kora.matrix.msu.edu/files/50/304/32-130-153D-84-Background_Paper_010_opt.pdf

Al Tamimi & Company. (2017). Employment & labour law in the UAE. Retrieved from http://www.lexology.com/library/detail.aspx?g=31e69b6a-4b6e-4f1d-8812-1843afdf5a0b

Alexander, M. (2012). *The new Jim Crow: Mass incarceration in the age of colorblindness*. New York, NY: The New Press.

Allen, T. E. (2012). *The invention of the white race: Vol. 1. Racial oppression and social control* (2nd ed.). New York, NY: Verso.

American Civil Liberties Union. (n.d.). *Voter's rights 2016: What's at stake*. Retrieved from https://www.aclu.org/issues/voting-rights/fighting-voter-suppression

American Indian Religious Freedom Act of 1978, 42 U.S.C. ch. 21, subch. I §§ 1996 & 1996a.

American Psychiatric Association. (2013). *Diagnostic and statistical manual of mental disorders* (5th ed.). Washington, DC: Author.

Americans With Disabilities Act of 1990, 42 U.S.C § 12101.

Anthias, F. (2001). The material and symbolic in theorizing social stratification: Issues of gender, ethnicity and class. *British Journal of Sociology, 52*(3), 367–390.

Appleby, G. A., Colon, E., & Hamilton, J. (2010). *Diversity, oppression and social functioning: Person-in-environment assessment and intervention* (3rd ed.). Boston, MA: Allyn & Bacon.

Aspen Institute. (2004). *Structural racism and community building*. Retrieved from https://assets.aspeninstitute.org/content/uploads/files/content/docs/rcc/aspen_structural_racism2.pdf

Ayvazian, A. (2001). Interrupting the cycle of oppression: The role of allies as agents of change. In P. S. Rothenberg (Ed.), *Race, class, and gender in the United States* (5th ed., pp. 609–615). New York, NY: Worth.

Baca Zinn, M., Hondagneu-Sotelo, Messner, M. A., & Denissen, A. M. (2016). *Gender through the prism of difference* (5th ed.). New York, NY: Oxford University Press.

Baines, D. (2000). Everyday practices of race, class and gender: Struggles, skills, and radical social work. *Journal of Progressive Human Services, 11*(2), 5–27.

Bambara, T. C. (1981). Foreword. In C. Moraga & G. Anzaldua (Eds.), *This bridge called my back: Writings by radical women of color* (pp. v–vii). Watertown, MA: Persephone Press.

Banks, J. A. (1997). *Educating citizens in a multicultural society.* New York, NY: Teachers College Press.

Barrientos, J., Silva, J., Catalan, S., Gómez, F., & Longueira, J. (2010). Discrimination and victimization: Parade for lesbian, gay, bisexual, and transgender (LGBT) pride in Chile. *Journal of Homosexuality, 57*(6), 760–775.

Bartlett, J. (1992). *Bartlett's familiar quotations* (16th ed.). Boston, MA: Little, Brown.

Bashford, A., & Levine, P. (2010). *The Oxford handbook of the history of eugenics.* New York, NY: Oxford University Press.

Bauman, J. (2005). How changing ads in health and fitness can change attitudes. Retrieved from http://ncpad.org/yourwrites/fact_sheet.php?sheet=243

Baynton, D. C. (2001). Disability and the justification of inequality in American history. In P. K. Longmore & L. Umansky (Eds.), *The new disability history: American perspectives* (pp. 33–58). New York, NY: New York University Press.

Begay, R. C., Roberts, R. N., Weisner, T. S., & Matheson, C. (1999). Indigenous and informal systems of support: Navajo families who have children with disabilities. *Bilingual Review, 24*(1/2), 79–94.

Bell, L. A. (1997). Theoretical foundations for social justice education. In M. Adams, L. A. Bell, & P. Griffin (Eds.), *Teaching for diversity and social justice: A sourcebook* (pp. 3–15). New York, NY: Routledge.

Bennett, J. M., & Bennett, M. J. (2004). Developing intercultural sensitivity: An integrative approach to global and domestic diversity. In D. Landis, J. Bennett, & M. Bennett (Eds.), *Handbook of intercultural training* (3rd ed., pp. 147–165). Thousand Oaks, CA: Sage.

Berman, S. L., You, Y., Schwartz, S., Teo, G., & Mochizuki, K. (2011). Identity exploration, commitment, and distress: A cross national investigation in China, Taiwan, Japan, and the United States. *Child Youth Care Forum, 40,* 65–75.

Bernasconi, R., & Lott, T. (Eds.). (2000). *The idea of race.* Indianapolis, IN: Hackett.

Besthorn, F. H. (2013). Radical equalitarian ecological justice: A social work call to action. In M. Gray, J. Coates, & T. Hetherington (Eds.), *Environmental social work* (pp. 31–45). New York, NY: Routledge.

Bettcher, T. M. (2007). Evil deceivers and make-believers: On transphobic violence and the politics of Illusion. *Hypatia: A Journal of Feminist Philosophy, 22*(3), 43–65.

Biddle, B. J. (1986). Recent developments in role theory. *Annual Review of Sociology, 12,* 67–92.

Bird, D. (2011). Aboriginal identity goes beyond skin color. *The Sydney Morning Herald.* Retrieved from http://www.smh.com.au/federal-politics/political-opinion/aboriginal-identity-goes-beyond-skin-colour-20110406-1d40r

Birkett, M., & Espelage, D. L. (2015). Homophobic name-calling, peer-groups, and masculinity: The socialization of homophobic behavior in adolescents. *Social Development, 24*(1), 184–205.

Bivens, D. (1995). *Internalized racism: A definition*. Retrieved from http://www. thewtc. org/Internalized_Racism.pdf

Block, P. (2009). *Community: The structure of belonging*. San Francisco, CA: Berrett-Koehler.

Bogdan, R. (1988). *Freak show: Presenting human oddities for amusement and profit*. Chicago, IL: University of Chicago Press.

Brockting, W. O. (2013).Transgender identity development. In D. L. Tolman et al. (Eds.), *American Psychological Association (APA) handbook of sexuality and psychology* (Vol. 1, pp. 739–748). Washington, DC: APA.

Brockting, W. O., & Coleman, E. (2007). Developmental stages of the transgender coming out process: Toward an integrated identity. In R. Ettner, S. Monstrey, & E. Eyler (Eds.), *Principles of transgender medicine and surgery* (pp. 185–208). New York, NY: Haworth Press.

Brookfield, S. (1995). *Becoming a Critically Reflective Teacher*. San Francisco: Jossey-Bass.

Brooks, F. (2000). Beneath contempt: The mistreatment of non-traditional/gender atypical boys. *Journal of Gay & Lesbian Social Services, 12*(1/2), 107–115.

Brown v. Board of Education of Topeka, 347 U.S. 483 (1954).

Bryson, V. (1999). *Feminist debates: Issues of theory and political practice*. New York, NY: New York University Press.

Buck v. Bell, 274 U.S.200 (1927).

Budgeon, S. (2011). The contradictions of successful femininity: Third-wave feminism, post feminism and "new" femininities. In R. Gill & C. Scarph (Eds.), *New femininities* (pp. 279–292). London, UK: Palgrave Macmillan.

Bullard, R. (Ed.). (1994). *Unequal protection*. San Francisco, CA: Sierra Club.

Burr, V. (1995). *Introduction to social constructionism*. New York, NY: Routledge.

Burr, V. (2015). *Social constructionism*. New York, NY: Routledge.

Butler, J. (1999). *Gender trouble: Feminism and the subversion of identity*. New York, NY: Routledge.

Butler, J. (2004). *Undoing gender*. New York, NY: Routledge.

Carter, R. T. (1995). *The influence of race and racial identity in psychotherapy*. New York, NY: John Wiley & Sons.

Caste system. (2017). In *New World Encyclopedia*. Retrieved from http://www. newworldencyclopedia.org/p/index.php?title=Caste_system&oldid=10027661

Castelli, L., Zogmaister, C., & Tomelleri, S. (2009). The transmission of racial attitudes within the family. *Developmental Psychology, 45*(2), 586–591.

Central Intelligence Agency (CIA). (2017). *The world factbook*. Retrieved from https:// www.cia.gov/library/publications/the-world-factbook/geos/in.html

Chandra, S. (2015). Spirituality in special education: A mirror of the ancient Indian society. *Indian Journal of Positive Psychology, 6*(3), 323–325.

Chavous, T. M., Bernat, D. H., Schmeelk-Cone, K., Caldwell, C. H., Kohn-Wood, L., & Zimmerman, M. A. (2003). Racial identity and academic attainment among African American adolescents. *Child Development, 74*, 1076–1090.

Chen, C., Duliani, J., & Piepzna-Samarasinha, L. L. (2011). *The revolution begins at home*. Brooklyn, NY: South End Press.

Cheng, M., & Berman, S. L. (2012). Globalization and identity development: A Chinese perspective. In S. J. Schwartz (Ed.), *Identity around the world. New directions for child and adolescent development, Number 138* (pp. 103–121). Hoboken, NJ: Wiley & Sons.

Chenowith, E., & Stephan, M. (2011). *Why civil resistance works: The strategic logic of nonviolent conflict*. New York, NY: Columbia University Press.

Chestang, L. W. (1972). *Character development in a hostile environment* (Occasional Paper No. 3). Chicago, IL: University of Chicago, School of Social Service Administration.

Chestang, L. W. (1984). Racial and personal identity in the black experience. In B.W. White (Ed.), *Color in a white society* (pp. 83–94). Silver Spring, MD: National Association of Social Workers.

Chinese Exclusion Act (1882). [Image of document]. *Our documents.* Retrieved from https://www.ourdocuments.gov/doc.php?flash=false&doc=47

Coates, J. (2003). *Ecology and social work: Toward a new paradigm.* Halifax, NS: Fernwood Books.

Coates, J. (2005). Environmental crisis: Implications for social work. *Journal of Progressive Human Services, 16*(1), 25–49.

Colling, S. (2010). Imaging transnational feminism (Blog post). Retrieved from https://transnationalfeminist.wordpress.com/2010/10/12/beyond-borders/

Collins, D., Falcón, S., Lodhia, S., & Talcott, M. (2010). New directions in feminism and human rights: An introduction. *International Feminist Journal of Politics, 12*(3–4), 298–318.

Collins, J. (2001). Level 5 leadership: The triumph of humility and fierce resolve. *Harvard Business Review, 79*(1), 66–76.

Columbia Law School. (2017). *Readings on citizenship and nationality in Israel/Palestine: Structures of identity, difference and democracy.* Retrieved from http://www.law.columbia.edu/open-university-project/curricula/citizenshipnationalityisrael-palestine

Conklin, J. (2006). *Dialogue mapping: Building shared understanding of wicked problems.* Chichester, UK: Wiley.

Cook, E. P. (1985). *Psychological androgyny.* New York, NY: Pergamon Press.

Cook, L., & Rosenberg, E. (2015). No one knows how many people died in Katrina. *US News and World Reports.* Retrieved from https://www.usnews.com/news/blogs/data-mine/2015/08/28/no-one-knows-how-many-people-died-in-katrina

Corbett, K. (1999). Homosexual boyhood: Notes on girl boys. In M. Rottnek (Ed.), *Sissies and tomboys: Gender nonconformity and homosexual childhood* (pp. 107–139). New York, NY: New York University Press.

Cranny-Francis, A., Waring, W. Stauropoulos, P., & Kirby, J. (2003). *Gender studies: Terms and debates.* New York, NY: Palgrave Macmillan.

Crass, C. (n.d.). *Beyond the whiteness—Global capitalism and white supremacy: thoughts on movement building and anti-racist organizing.* Retrieved from http://www.coloursofresistance.org/492/beyond-the-whiteness-global-capitalism-and-white-supremacy-thoughts-on-movement-building-and-anti-racist-organizing/

Crenshaw, K. (1989). Demarginalizing the intersection of race and sex: A black feminist critique of antidiscrimination doctrine, feminist theory and antiracist politics. *The University of Chicago Legal Forum, 140,* 139–167.

Crenshaw, K. (1991). Mapping the margins: Intersectionality, identity politics, and violence against women of color. *Stanford Law Review, 43*(6), 1241–1299. Retrieved from http://www.jstor.org/stable/1229039

Crenshaw, K. (2014). Kimberlé Crenshaw on intersectionality: "I wanted to come up with an everyday metaphor that anyone could use." Retrieved from http://www.newstatesman.com/lifestyle/2014/04/kimberl-crenshaw-intersectionality-i-wanted-come-everyday-metaphor-anyone-could

Croskerry, P., Singhal, G., & Mamede, S. (2013). Cognitive debiasing 2: Impediments to and strategies for change. *BMJ Quality & Safety, 22*(6), 5–72. Retrieved from http://qualitysafety.bmj.com/content/22/Suppl_2/ii65

Cross, S. L., & Day, A. G. (2017). American Indians' response to physical pain: Functional limitations and help-seeking behaviors. In H. N. Weaver & F. K. Yuen (Eds.), *All my relations: Understanding the experiences of Native Americans with disabilities* (pp. 176–191). New York, NY: Routledge.

Cross, W. (1978). The Thomas and Cross models of psychological Nigrescence: A literature review. *Journal of Black Psychology, 5*(1), 13–31.

Cross, W. E. (1980). Models of psychological Nigrescence: A literature review. In R. L. Jones (Ed.), *Black psychology* (2nd ed., pp. 81–89). New York, NY: Harper & Row.

Cross, W. E. (1991). *Shades of black: Diversity in African-American identity.* Philadelphia, PA: Temple University Press.

Cross, W. E. (1995). The psychology of Nigrescence: Revising the Cross model. In J. G. Ponterotto, J. M. Casas, L. A. Suzuki, & C. M. Alexander (Eds.), *Handbook of multicultural counseling* (pp. 93–122). Thousand Oaks, CA: Sage.

Cudd, A. (2006). *Analyzing oppression.* Oxford, UK: Oxford University Press.

Cuomo, C. (2003). *The philosopher queen: Feminist essays on war, love and knowledge.* Lanham, MD: Rowman & Littlefield.

Currah, P., & Minter, S. (2000). *Transgender equality: A handbook for activists and policymakers.* Washington, DC: National Gay and Lesbian Task Force.

Curry-Stevens, A. (2005). *Pedagogy for the privileged: Transformation processes and ethical dilemmas.* Paper delivered at the twenty-fourth annual conference of the Canadian Association for the Study of Adult Education, London, Ontario.

Dalton, H. (2002). Failing to see. In P. Rothenberg (Ed.), *White privilege: Essential readings on the other side of racism* (pp. 15–18). New York, NY: Worth.

DasGupta, K. (2015). *Introducing social stratification: The causes and consequences of inequality.* Boulder, CO: Lynne Rienner.

Dasgupta, N. (2013). Implicit attitudes and beliefs adapt to situations: A decade of research on the malleability of implicit prejudice, stereotypes, and the self-concept. *Advances in Experimental Social Psychology, 47,* 233–279.

Davis, K., & Moore, W. (1945). *Some principles of stratification. American Sociological Review, 10*(2), 242–249.

Davis, L. J. (2016). Introduction: Normality, power and culture. In L. J. Davis (Ed.), *The disability studies reader* (5th ed.). New York, NY: Routledge.

Dawson, M. C. (2001). *Black visions: The roots of contemporary African-American political ideologies.* Chicago, IL: University of Chicago Press.

D'Cruz, H. D., Gillingham, P., & Melendez, S. (2015). Reflexivity, its meanings and relevance for social work: A critical review of the literature. *British Journal of Social Work, 37,* 73–90. Retrieved from https://www.researchgate.net/publication/ 31343854_

Delgado, R., & Stefancic, J. (2017). *Critical race theory.* New York, NY: NYU Press.

Devore, W., & Schlesinger, E. G. (1998). *Ethnic-sensitive social work practice* (5th ed.). Boston, MA: Allyn & Bacon.

Dirks, N. B. (2001). *Castes of mind: Colonialism and the making of India.* Princeton, NJ: Princeton University Press.

Doob, C. B. (2016). *Social inequality and social stratification in U.S. society.* New York, NY: Routledge.

Dreyfus, T. (2012). The "half-invention" of gender identity in international human rights law: From cedaw to the yogyakarta principles. *Australian Feminist Law Journal, 37*(1), 33–50.

Education For All handicapped Children Act, 20 U.S.C. §§ 1400–1461 (1982 & Supp. III 1985).

Ehrenreich, B., & Hochschild, A. R. (2016). Global woman. In M. Baca Zinn, P. Hondagneu-Sotelo, M. A. Messner, & A. M. Denissen. (Eds.), *Gender through the prism of difference* (5th ed., pp. 53–59). New York, NY: Oxford University Press.

Ellis, H. B., & Abdi, S. (2017). Building community resilience to violent extremism through genuine partnerships. *American Psychologist, 72*(3), 289–300.

Embassy of the United Arab Emirates. (2017). *Labor rights in the UAE.* Retrieved from http://www.uae-embassy.org/about-uae/human-rights/labor-rights-uae

Erikson, E. H. (1968). *Identity, youth and crisis.* New York, NY: W. W. Norton.

Esri, M. K. (2013). Where are the 50 most populous refugee camps? *SmithsonianMag.* Retrieved from http://www.smithsonianmag.com/innovation/where-are-50-most-populous-refugee-camps-180947916/

Faircloth, S. C. (2006). Early childhood education among Native American/Alaskan Native children with disabilities: Implications for research and practice. *Rural Special Education Quarterly, 25*(1), 25–31.

Faludi, S. (2006*). Backlash: The undeclared war against American women* (15th ed.). New York, NY: Three Rivers Press.

Fausto-Sterling, A. (1992). *Myths of gender: Biological theories about women and men.* New York, NY: Basic Books.

Ferdman, B. M., & Gallegos, P. I. (2001). Racial identity development and Latinos in the United States. In C. L. Wijeyesinghe & B. W. Jackson III (Eds.), *New perspectives on racial identity development: A theoretical and practical anthology* (pp. 32–66). New York, NY: New York University Press.

Fook, J. (1999). Critical reflectivity in education and practice. In B. Pease & J. Fook (Eds.), *Transforming social work practice: postmodern critical perspectives* (pp. 195–208). St Leonards, Australia: Allen and Unwin.

Fredrickson, G. M., & Camarillo, A. (2015). *Racism: A short history (Princeton classics).* Princeton, NJ: Princeton University Press.

Freire, P. (1970). *Pedagogy of the Oppressed.* New York: Herder and Herder.

Freire, P. (1985). *Pedagogy of the oppressed.* New York, NY: Continuum.

Freire, P. (1991). The importance of the act of reading. In C. Mitchell & K. Weiler (Eds.), *Rewriting literacy: Culture and the discourse of the other* (pp. 139–145). Westport, CT: Bergin & Garvey.

Freire, P. (1997). *Pedagogy of the heart.* New York, NY: Continuum.

Freire, P. (2000). *Pedagogy of the oppressed* (30th Anniversary ed.). New York, NY: Continuum.

Friedman, T. L. (2006). *The world is flat: A brief history of the twenty-first century.* New York, NY: Farrar, Straus and Giroux.

Frye, M. (1983). *The politics of reality: Oppression.* Retrieved from https://feministtheoryreadinggroup.wordpress.com/2010/11/23/marilyn-frye-the-politics-of-reality-oppression/

Frye, M. (2000). Oppression. In P. S. Rothenberg (Ed.), *Race, class, and gender in the United States: An integrated study* (5th ed., pp. 139–142). New York. NY: Worth.

Gainor, K. A. (2000). Including transgender issues in lesbian, gay, and bisexual psychology: Implications for clinical practice and training. In B. Greene & G. L. Croom (Eds.), *Education, research, and practice in lesbian, gay, bisexual, and transgendered psychology: A resource manual* (pp. 131–160). Thousand Oaks, CA: Sage.

Galtung, J. (1990. Cultural violence. *Journal of Peace Research, 27*(3), 291–305. Retrieved from http://www.jstor.org/stable/423472

Garbarino, J. (1999). *Lost boys: Why our sons turn violent and how we can save them.* New York, NY: Anchor Books.

Garland, R. (1995). *The eye of the beholder: Deformity and disability in the Greco-Roman world*. Ithaca, NY: Cornell University Press.

Garnets, L. D. (2002). Sexual orientations in perspective. *Cultural Diversity and Ethnic Minority Psychology, 8*(2), 115–129.

Garnets, L. D., & Peplau, L. A. (2001). A new paradigm for women's sexual orientation: Implications for therapy. *Women & Therapy, 24*(1/2), 111–121.

Gayer, L. (2000). The globalization of identity politics: The Sikh experience. *International Journal of Punjab Studies, 7*(2), 223–262.

Georgetown University. (n.d.). The Nazi eugenics programs. In *High school bioethics curriculum project* (Chapter 5). Retrieved from https://highschoolbioethics.georgetown.edu/units/cases/unit4_5.html

Gergen, K. J. (2011). The social construction of self. In S. Ghallager (Ed.), *The Oxford handbook of self* (pp. 633–653). Retrieved from http://www.oxfordhandbooks.com/view/10.1093/oxfordhb/9780199548019.001.0001/oxfordhb-9780199548019-e-28

Gil, D. G. (1998). *Confronting injustice and oppression: Concepts and strategies for social workers*. New York, NY: Columbia University Press.

Girlin, T. (1994). From universality to difference. In C. Calhoun, (Ed.), *Social theory and the politics of identity* (pp. 150–174). Cambridge, MA: Blackwell.

Giroux, H. A. (1993). Literacy and the politics of difference. In C. Lankshear & P. L. McLaren (Eds.), *Critical literacy: Politics, praxis, and the postmodern* (pp. 367–378). Albany, NY: State University of New York.

Giroux, H. A. (1997). *Pedagogy and the politics of hope: Theory, culture, and schooling*. Boulder, CO: Westview Press.

Giroux, H. A. (2011). *On critical pedagogy*. New York, NY: Bloomsbury.

Goodley, D. (2012). Dis/entangling critical disability studies. *Disability and Society, 28*(5), 631–644.

Goodman, D. J. (2015). Oppression and privilege: Two sides of the same coin. *Journal of Intercultural Communication, 18*, 1–14. Retrieved from http://www.dianegoodman.com/PrivilegeandOppression

Gradin, C. (2010). *Race and income distribution: Evidence from the US, Brazil and South Africa*. Retrieved from http://www.ecineq.org/milano/wp/ecineq2010-179.pdf

The Green Belt Movement. (n.d.). Retrieved from http://www.greenbeltmovement.org

Greene, B. (2000). Beyond heterosexism and across the cultural divide: Developing an inclusive lesbian, gay, and bisexual psychology: A look to the future. In B. Greene & G. L. Croom (Eds.), *Education, research, and practice in lesbian, gay, bisexual, and transgendered psychology: A resource manual* (pp. 1–45). Thousand Oaks, CA: Sage.

Greene, M. L., Way, N., & Pahl, K. (2006). Trajectories of perceived adult and peer discrimination among black, Latino, and Asian American adolescents: Patterns and psychological correlates. *Developmental Psychology, 42*, 218–236.

Grossman, A. H., & D'Augelli, A. R. (2006). Transgender youth: Invisible and vulnerable. *Journal of Homosexuality, 51*(1), 111–128.

Hammer, M. (2012). The Intercultural Development Inventory: A new frontier in assessment and development of intercultural competence. In M. Vande Berg, R. M. Paige, & K. H. Lou (Eds.), *Student learning abroad* (Ch. 5, pp. 115–136). Sterling, VA: Stylus.

Hammer, M. R. (2011). Additional cross-cultural validity testing of the Intercultural Development Inventory. *International Journal of Intercultural Relations, 35*, 474–487.

Hancock, K. A. (2000). Lesbian, gay, and bisexual lives: Basic issues in psychotherapy training and practice. In B. Greene & G. L. Croom (Eds.), *Education, research, and practice in lesbian, gay, bisexual, and transgendered psychology: A resource manual* (pp. 91–130). Thousand Oaks, CA: Sage.

Handrahan, L. (2002). *Gendering ethnicity.* New York, NY: Taylor & Francis.

Hardiman, R., & Jackson, B. W. (1997). Conceptual foundations for social justice courses. In M. Adams, L. A. Bell, & P. Griffin (Eds.), *Teaching for diversity and social justice: A sourcebook* (pp. 30–43). New York, NY: Routledge.

Hardiman, R., Jackson, B., & Griffin, P. (2007). Conceptual foundations for social justice courses. In M. Adams, L. A. Bell, & P. Griffin (Eds.), *Teaching for diversity and social justice* (2nd ed., pp. 35–66). New York, NY: Routledge.

Hatton, N., & Smith, D. (1995). Reflection in teacher education: Towards definition and implementation. *Teaching and Teacher Education, 11*(1), 33–49. Retrieved from http://www.academia.edu/8696081/Reflection_in_teacher_education_ Towards_definition_and_implementation

Haynes, D. (2015). Effects of Hurricane Katrina still visible 10 years later. *United Press International (UPI).* Retrieved from https://www.upi.com/Top_News/ US/2015/08/29/Effects-of-Hurricane-Katrina-still-visible-10-years-later/ 5581440167964/

Helms, J. E. (1984). Toward an explanation of the influence of race in the counseling process: A black-white model. *Counseling Psychologist, 12*, 153–165.

Helms, J. E. (1993a). Applying the interaction model to social dyads. In J. E. Helms (Ed.), *Black and white racial identity* (pp. 177–185). Westport, CT: Praeger.

Helms, J. E. (1993b). The beginnings of a diagnostic model of racial identity. In J. E. Helms (Ed.), *Black and white racial identity* (pp. 83–104). Westport, CT: Praeger.

Helms, J. E. (Ed.). (1993c). *Black and white racial identity.* Westport, CT: Praeger.

Helms, J. E. (1993d).Toward a model of white racial identity development. In J. E. Helms (Ed.), *Black and white racial identity* (pp. 49–66). Westport, CT: Praeger.

Helms, J. E. (1994). Racial identity and racial constructs. In E. J. Trickett, R. Watts, & D. Birman (Eds.), *Human diversity* (pp. 285–311). San Francisco, CA: Jossey-Bass.

Helms, J. E. (2015). Taking action against racism in a post-racism era: The origins and almost demise of an idea. *Counseling Psychologist, 43*, 138–145.

Henrique, G. (2016). *Self-reflective awareness: A crucial life skill* [Web log post]. Retrieved from https://www.psychologytoday.com/blog/theory-knowledge/201609/ self-reflective-awareness-crucial-life-skill

Herek, G. M. (Ed.). (1998). *Stigma and sexual orientation: Understanding prejudice against lesbians, gay men, and bisexuals.* Thousand Oaks, CA: Sage.

Hering Torres, M. S. (2012). Purity of blood: Problems of interpretations. In M. S. Torres, M. E. Martinez, & D. Nirenberg (Eds.). *Race and blood in the Iberian world.* Zurich, Switzerland: Lit Verlag.

Hinduism and homosexuality. (2016). *Religion facts.* Retrieved from http://www. religionfacts.com/homosexuality/hinduism

Hoard, W. B. (1973). *Anthology: Quotations and sayings of people of color.* San Francisco, CA: R and E Research Associates.

Holland Bloorview Hospital. (2016). *A future of possibilities.* Retrieved from http://hollandbloorview.ca/newsarticle/Holland-Bloorview-challenges- Canadians-to-rethink-childhood-disability-

Holland, T. P., & Kilpatrick, A. C. (1993). Using narrative techniques to enhance multicultural practice. *Journal of Social Work Education, 29*(3), 302–308.

Holvino, E. (2012). The "simultaneity" of identities: Model and skills for the twenty-first century. In C. L. Wijeyesinghe & B. W. Jackson III (Eds.), *New perspectives on racial identity development: Integrating emerging frameworks* (2nd ed., pp. 81–107). New York, NY: New York University Press.

hooks, b. (1994). *Teaching to transgress: Education as the practice of freedom.* London, UK: Routledge.

hooks, b. (1995). *Killing rage: Ending racism.* New York, NY: Henry Holt.

hooks, b. (1997). Sisterhood: political solidarity between women. In Anne McClintock, Mufti, Aamir; & Shohat, Ella (Eds.), *Dangerous liaisons: gender, nation, and post-colonial perspectives* (pp. 396–414). Minnesota, Minneapolis: University of Minnesota Press.

hooks, b. (2009). *belonging: a culture of place.* New York, NY: Routledge.

hooks, b. [ChallengingMedia]. (2006,). *Cultural criticism and transformation* [video file]. Retrieved from https://www.youtube.com/watch?v=zQUuHFKP-9s

hooks, b. (2015). *Feminism is for everybody: Passionate politics.* New York, NY: Routledge.

Hughes, L. (1994). *The collected poems of Langston Hughes.* New York, NY: Knopf.

Human Rights Campaign. (n.d.) *Stances of faiths on LGBTQ issues: Buddhism.* Retrieved from http://www.hrc.org/resources/stances-of-faiths-on-lgbt-issues-buddhism

Human Rights Watch. (2010a).Disability rights. Retrieved from https://www.hrw.org/topic/disability-rights

Human Rights Watch. (2001b). *Caste discrimination: A global concern.* [Report by Human Rights Watch for the United Nations world conference against racism, racial discrimination, xenophobia and related intolerance]. Retrieved from https://www.hrw.org/reports/2001/globalcaste/caste0801.pdf

Human Rights Watch. (2011c). *Sterilization of women and girls with disabilities: A briefing paper.* Retrieved from https://www.hrw.org/news/2011/11/10/sterilization-women-and-girls-disabilities

Hutchinson, A-M. K., Stuart, A. D., & Pretorius, H. G. (2010). Biological contributions to well-being: The relationships amongst temperament, character strengths and resilience. *South African Journal of Industrial Psychology, 36*(2), 1–10.

Ignatiev, N. (2009). *How the Irish became white.* New York, NY: Routledge.

ILGA. (2017). State sponsored homophobia. Retrieved on August 1, 2017 from http://ilga.org/downloads/2017/ILGA_State_Sponsored_Homophobia_2017_WEB.pdf

Income Inequality. (n.d.). Retrieved from https://inequality.org/facts/income-inequality/

Intercultural Development Inventory (IDI). (n.d.) *The Intercultural Development Continuum (IDC).* Retrieved from https://idiinventory.com/products/the-intercultural-development-continuum-idc/

Intergovernmental Panel on Climate Change (IPCC). (2015). *Climate change 2014: Mitigation of climate change: Summary for policymakers.* Retrieved from https://www.ipcc.ch/pdf/assessment-report/ar5/wg3/WGIIIAR5_SPM_TS_Volume.pdf

International Dalit Solidarity Network. (n.d.). *Caste discrimination.* Retrieved from http://idsn.org/caste-discrimination

International Food Policy Research Institute. (2015). *Global nutrition report.* Retrieved from http://ebrary.ifpri.org/utils/getfile/collection/p15738coll2/id/129443/filename/129654.pdf

International Organization for Migration (IOM). (n.d.). *Migration and climate change: What are the estimates?* Retrieved from https://www.iom.int/migration-and-climate-change-0

James, M. (2016). Race. In Edward N. Zalta (Ed.). *The Stanford encyclopedia of philosophy.* Retrieved from http://plato.stanford.edu/archives/spr2016/entries/race/

Jenson, R. (1998). Mens's lives and feminist theory. In K. Conway-Turner, S. Cherrin, J. Shiffman, & K. D. Turkel (Eds.), *Women's studies in transition: The pursuit of interdisciplinary* (pp. 19–33). Cranbury, NH: Associated University Presses.

Jobson, G. A., Theron, L. B., Kaggwa, J. K., & Kim, H. J. (2012). Transgender in Africa: Invisible, inaccessible, or ignored? *SAHARA-J: Journal of Social Aspects of HIV/AIDS, 9*(3), 160–163.

Judge, P. S., & Bal, G. (2008). Understanding the paradox of changes among Dalits in Punjab. *Economic and Political Weekly, 43*(41), 11 October, 49–55.

Just Conflict. (n.d.). *Systems of oppression.* Retrieved on June 23, 2017, from http://www.creativeconflictresolution.org/jc/maps-1/systems-of-oppression.html

Kahn, S. (1991). *Organizing: A guide for grassroots leaders* (Rev.ed.). Washington, DC: NASW Press.

Kanpol, B. (1997). *Issues and trends in critical pedagogy.* Cresskill, NJ: Hampton Press.

Karp, D. (2010). Unlocking men, unmasking masculinities: Doing men's work in prison. *Journal of Men's Studies, 18*(1), 63–83.

Keenan, E. K. (2004). From sociocultural categories to socially located relations: Using critical theory in social work practice. *Families in Society, 85*(4), 539–548.

Kezar, A. (2002). Reconstructing static images of leadership: An application of positionality theory. *Journal of Leadership Studies, 8*(3), 94–109.

Khaleej Times. (2016). *Clash of minimum wages affects hiring of Indians in UAE.* Retrieved from http://www.khaleejtimes.com/nation/general/clash-of-minimum-wages-affects-hiring-of-indians-in-uae

Kich, G. K. (1992). The developmental process of asserting a biracial, bicultural identity. In M. P. P. Root (Ed.), *Racially mixed people in America* (pp. 263–276). Thousand Oaks, CA: Sage.

Kim, J. (2001). Asian American identity development theory. In C. L. Wijeyesinghe & B. W. Jackson III (Eds.), *New perspectives on racial identity development: A theoretical and practical anthology* (pp. 67–90). New York, NY: New York University Press.

Kincheloe, J. & Steinberg, S. R. (1997). *Changing multiculturalism.* Philadelphia, PA: Open University Press.

King-O'Riain, R. C., & Small, S. (2014). Introduction. In R. C. King-O'Riain, S. Small, M. Mahtani, M. Song, & P. Spickard (Eds.). *Global mixed race* (pp. Vii–xxii). New York, NY: New York University Press.

Knight, S. (2012). Debt-bondage slavery in India. *Global Dialogue, 14*(2), 62–72.

Kokemail, P. & de Lange, F. P. (2014). Shape perception simultaneously up-and down regulates neural activity in the primary visual cortex. *Current Biology.* doi:10.1016/j.cub.2014.05.042.

Kondrat, M. E. (1999). Who is the "self" in self-aware: Professional self-awareness from a critical theory perspective. *Social Service Review, 73*(4), 451–477.

Kouzes, J. & Posner, B. (2017). *The leadership challenge: How to make extraordinary things happen in organizations.* San Francisco, CA: Jossey-Bass.

Kudlick, C. (2003). Disability history: Why we need another "other." *American Historical Review, 108*(3), 763–793.

Lafromboise, T., Coleman, H. L. K., & Gerton, J. (1993). Psychological impact of biculturalism: Evidence and theory. *Psychological Bulletin, 114*(3), 395–412.

Lam, C. (1997). A cultural perspective on the study of Chinese adolescent development. *Child and Adolescent Social Work Journal, 14*(2), 95–113.

Lederach, J. P., & Lederach, A. J. (2010). *When blood and bones cry out: Journeys thro the soundscape of healing and reconciliation*. Oxford, UK: Oxford University Pro

Leigh, J. W. (1998). *Communicating for cultural competence*. Prospect Heights, IL: Waveland Press.

Lie, G.-Y., & Lowery, C. T. (2003). Cultural competence with women of color. In D. Lum (Ed.), *Culturally competent practice: A framework for understanding diverse groups and justice issues* (2nd ed., pp. 282–309). Pacific Grove, CA: Brooks/Cole.

Lindsey, L. L. (2016). *Gender roles: A sociological perspective* (6th ed.). New York, NY: Routledge.

Lippa, R.A. (2005). *Gender, nature, and nurture* (2nd ed.). New York, NY: Taylor & Frances.

Lips, H. M. (2017). *A new psychology of women: Gender, culture, and ethnicity* (4th ed.) Long Grove, IL: Waveland Press.

Lombardi, E., & Bettcher, T. (2005). Lesbian, gay, bisexual, and transgender/transsexual individuals. In B. Levy & V. Sidel (Eds.), *Social injustice and public health* (pp. 130–144). New York, NY: Oxford University Press.

Lopez, I. F. (1996). *White by law: The legal construction of race*. New York, NY: New York University Press.

López, I. H. (2006). *White by Law 10th Anniversary Edition: The Legal Construction of Race*. New York: New York University Press.

Lorde, A. (1983). There is no hierarchy of oppressions. *Interracial Books for Children Bulletin, 14*(3/4), 9.

Lorde, A. (2007). *Sister outsider: Essays and speeches*. Freedom, CA: Crossing Press.

Lorde, A. (2016). Age, race, class, and sex: Women refining difference. In M. Baca Zinn, P. Hondagneu-Sotelo, M. A. Messner, & A. M. Denissen (Eds.), *Gender through the prism of difference* (5th ed., pp. 270–274). New York, NY: Oxford University Press.

Loving v. Virginia, 388 U.S. 1 (1967).

Lowe, C. (2001). The trouble with tribe. *Teaching Tolerance Magazine, 19*. Retrieved from http://www.tolerance.org/magazine/number-19-spring-2001/feature/trouble-tribe

Lum, D. (2010, June). *Culturally competent practice: A framework for understanding diverse groups and justice issues* (4th ed.). Pacific Grove, CA: Brooks/Cole.

Maalouf, A. (2012). *In the name of identity: Violence and the need to belong* (B. Bray, Trans.). New York, NY: Arcade. (Original work published 1996)

Maathai, W. (2003). *The Green Belt Movement: Sharing the approach and the experience*. New York, NY: Lantern Books.

Maathai, W. (n.d). Wangari Maathai Quotes. Retrieved from https://www.goodreads.com/quotes/164567-human-rights-are-not-things-that-are-put-on-the

Mackelprang, R., & Salsgiver, R. (1999). *Disability: A diversity model approach in human service practice*. Pacific Grove, CA: Brooks/Cole.

MacRae, A., & Zehr, H. (2004). *The little book of family group conferences: New Zealand style*. Intercourse, PA: Good Books.

Maguire, P. (1987). *Doing participatory research: A feminist approach*. Amherst, MA: Center for International Education.

Maher, F. A., & Tetreatult, M. K. (1993). Frames of positionality: Constructing meaningful dialogues about gender and race. *Anthropological Quarterly, 66*(3), 118–127.

Mallon, G. P. (1999a). A call for organizational trans-formation. *Journal of Gay and Lesbian Social Services, 10*(3/4), 131–142.

Mallon, G. P. (1999b). Knowledge for practice with transgendered persons. *Journal of Gay and Lesbian Social Services, 10*(3/4), 1–18.

Mallon, G. P. (1999c). Practice with transgendered children. *Journal of Gay and Lesbian Social Services, 10*(3/4), 49–64.

Mand, K. (2006). Gender, ethnicity and social relations in the narratives of elderly Sikh men and women. *Ethnic and Racial Studies, 29*(6), 1057–1071.

Mandela, N. (1994). *The long walk to freedom: Autobiography of Nelson Mandela.* Boston, MA: Back Bay Books.

Marger, M. N. (1997). *Race and ethnic relations: American and global perspectives.* Belmont, CA: Wadsworth.

Marsh, J. C. (2004). Social work in a multicultural society. *Social Work, 49*(1), 5–6.

May, V. M. (2015). *Pursuing intersectionality, Unsettling dominant imaginaries.* London, UK: Routledge.

McLaren, P. (1997). *Revolutionary multiculturalism: Pedagogies of dissent for the new millennium.* Boulder, CO: Westview Press.

McMichael, P. (2017). *Development and social change* (6th ed.). Los Angeles, CA: Sage.

McPhatter, A. R. (1997). Cultural competence in child welfare: What is it? How do we achieve it? What happens without it? *Child Welfare, 76*(1), 255–278.

McPhatter, A. R., & Ganaway, T. L. (2003). Beyond the rhetoric: Strategies for implementing culturally effective practice with children, families, and communities. *Child Welfare, 82*(2), 103–125.

Mehrotra, N. (2013). *Disability, gender & state policy: Exploring margins.* Jawahar, Jaipur, India: Rawat Publications.

Mekawi, Y., Bresin, K., & Hunter, C. D. (2015). White fear, dehumanization, and low empathy: lethal combinations for shooting bias. *Cultural Diversity and Ethnic Minority Psychology, 3.* doi:10.1037/cdp0000067.

Melamed, C. (2012). Gender is just one of many inequalities that generate poverty and exclusion. *The Guardian.* Retrieved from https://www.theguardian.com/global-development/poverty-matters/2012/mar/09/gender-inequality-poverty-exclusion

Menjivar, C. (2016). A framework for examining violence. In M. Baca Zinn, M. Hondagneu-Sotelo, M. A. Messner, & A. M. Denissen (Eds.), *Gender through the prism of difference* (5th ed., pp. 130–144). New York, NY: Oxford University Press.

Mental Health Parity Act of 1996, 29 U.S.C. § 1185a.

Merriam, S. B., Johnson-Bailey, J., Lee, M/Y., Lee, M. Y., Lee, Y., Ntseane, G., & Muhamed, M. (2001). Power and positionality: Negotiating insider/outsider status within and across cultures. *International Journal of Lifelong Education, 20*(5), 405–416.

Merton, L., & Dater, A. (Directors and Producers). (2008). *Taking root: the vision of Wangari Maathari* [Motion picture]. United States: Marlboro Productions.

Metz, I., Ng, E. S., Cornelius, N., Hoobler, J. M., & Nkimo, S. (2014). A comparative review of multiculturalism in Australia, Canada, the United Kingdom, the United States and South Africa. In A. Klarsfeld, E. S. Ng, L. A. E. Booysen, L. C. Christiansen, & B. Kuvaan (Eds.). *Comparative perspectives in diversity management.* Cheltenham, UK: Edgar Elgar.

Meyer, J. W. (1994). The evolution of modern stratification systems. In D. B. Grusky (Ed.), *Social stratification: Class, race, and gender in sociological perspective* (pp. 730–737). Boulder, CO: Westview Press.

Michalko, R. (2002). *The difference that disability makes.* Philadelphia, PA: Temple University Press.

Milkie, M. A. (2002). Contested images of femininity: An analysis of cultural gatekeepers and struggles with the "real girl" critique. *Gender and Society, 16*(6), 839–859.

Miller, D. B., & MacIntosh, R. (1999). Promoting resilience in urban African American adolescents: Racial socialization and identity. *Social Work Research, 23*(3), 159–170.

Miville, M. L. (2005). Psychological functioning and identity development of biracial people: A review of current theory and research. In R. T. Carter (Ed.), *Handbook of racial-cultural psychology and counseling* (pp. 295–319). Hoboken, NJ: Wiley.

Miville, M. L., Constantine, M. G., Baysden, M. F., & So-Lloyd, G. (2005). Chameleon changes: An exploration of racial identity themes of multiracial people. *Journal of Counseling Psychology, 52*, 507–516.

Moghadam, V. (2015). Gender and globalization: Female labor and women's mobilization. *Journal of World-Systems Research, 5*(2), 366–389.

Mohanty, C. T. (2003). *Feminism without borders: Decolonizing theory, practicing solidarity*. Durham, NC: Duke University Press.

Moi, T. (1999). *What is a woman? And other essays*. New York, NY: Oxford University Press.

Molloy, P. M. (2014). Debunking the myths: Transgender health & well-being. *The Advocate*. Retrieved from https://www.advocate.com/politics/transgender/2014/03/13/watch-debunking-surgery-top-priority-trans-people-myth

Moore, S. E., Adedoyin, A. C., & Robinson, M. A. (2017). *Police and the unarmed black male crisis: Advancing effective prevention strategies*. London, UK: Taylor & Francis.

Moosa-Mitha, M., & Ross-Sheriff, F. (2010). Transnational social work and lessons learned from transnational feminism. *Affilia: Journal of Women and Social Work, 25*(2), 105–107.

Moss, M. P., Schell, M. C., & Goins, R. T. (2006). Using GIS in the first national mapping of functional disability among older American Indians and Alaska natives from the 2000 census. *International Journal of Health Geographics, 5*(37), 37–48.

Mullaly, B. (2002). *Challenging oppression: A critical social work approach*. Toronto, ON: Oxford University Press.

Mullaly, B. (2010). *Challenging oppression and confronting privilege* (2nd ed.). New York, NY: Oxford University Press.

Munyi, C. (2012). Past and present perceptions towards disability: A historical perspective. *Disability Studies Quarterly, 32*(2). doi:10.18061/dsq.v32i2.3197

Muro, D., & Guiroga, A. (2005). Spanish nationalism: Ethnic or chic? *Ethnicities, 5*(1), 9–29. Retrieved from https://www.academia.edu/556970/Spanish_Nationalism_Ethnic_or_Civic_2005_

Nadal, K. L., Wong, U. Y., Griffin, D., Sriken, J., Vargas, V., Wideman, M., & Kolawole, A. (2010). Microaggressions and the multiracial experience. *International Journal of Humanities and Social Sciences, 1*, 36–44.

Nagar, R. (2002). Footloose researchers, "traveling" theories, and the politics of transnational feminist praxis. *Gender, Place and Culture, 9*, 179–186.

National Center for Transgender Equality. (n.d.). *Issues: Non-discrimination laws*. Retrieved from http://www.transequality.org/issues/non-discrimination-laws

Ndubuisi, F. O. (2013). The philosophical paradigm of African identity and development. *Open Journal of Philosophy, 3*(1A), 222–230.

Neela, G., & Knight, K. (2016). *Rights in transition: Making legal recognition for transgender people a global priority*. Retrieved from https://www.hrw.org/world-report/2016/rights-in-transition

Ngan-ling, E. (1996). Introduction. Transforming knowledge: Race, class, and gender. In E. N. Chow, D. Wilkinson, & M. B. Zinn (Eds.), *Race, class, and gender: Common bonds, different voices* (pp. ix–xix). Thousand Oaks, CA: Sage.

Nielson, K. (2013). *A disability history of the United States.* Boston, MA: Beacon Press.

Nolen, S. (2015). Brazil's colour blind. *The Globe and Mail.* Retrieved from https://www.theglobeandmail.com/news/world/brazils-colour-bind/article25779474/

Northway, R. (1997). Disability and oppression: Some implications for nurses and nursing. *Journal of Advanced Nursing, 26,* 736–743.

Olson, J. (2004). *The abolition of white democracy.* Minneapolis: University of Minnesota Press.

O'Neil, D. (2010). *Culture specific diseases.* Retrieved from http://anthro.palomar.edu/medical/med_4.htm

Onwuachi-Willig, A. (2013). *According to our hearts: Rhinelander v. Rhinelander and the law of the multiracial family.* New Haven, CT: Yale University Press.

Onwuachi-Willig, A. (2016). Race and racial identity are social constructs. *New York Times.* Retrieved from https://www.nytimes.com/roomfordebate/2015/06/16/how-fluid-is-racial-identity/race-and-racial-identity-are-social-constructs

Organization for Economic Cooperation and Development. (2013). *Government at a Glance: Norway.* Retrieved from https://www.oecd.org/gov/Norway.pdf

Outreach Program on the Rwanda Genocide and the United Nations. (2012). *The justice and reconciliation process in Rwanda.* Retrieved from http://www.un.org/en/preventgenocide/rwanda/pdf/bgjustice.pdf

OXFAM. (2016). *An economy for the 1%: How privilege and power in the economy drive extreme inequality and how this can be stopped.* Retrieved from https://policy-practice.oxfam.org.uk/publications/an-economy-for-the-1-how-privilege-and-power-in-the-economy-drive-extreme-inequ-592643

OXFAM. (2017). *Even it up: 8 men own same wealth as half the world.* Retrieved from https://www.oxfam.org/en/pressroom/pressreleases/2017-01-16/just-8-men-own-same-wealth-half-world

Paniagua, F. A. (2000). Culture-bound syndromes, cultural variations, and psychopathology. In I. Cuéllar & F. A. Paniagua (Eds.), *Handbook of multicultural mental health: Assessment and treatment of diverse populations* (pp. 140–141). New York, NY: Academic Press.

Pardo, S. T. (2008). *ACT for (Trans) youth, part 1. Growing up transgender: Research and theory.* Retrieved from http://www.actforyouth.net/resources/rf/rf_trans-identity_0308.pdf

Parsons, T. (1951). *Social system: The major exposition of the author's conceptual scheme for the analysis of the dynamics of the social system.* London, UK: Routledge & Kegan Paul.

Patten, E. (2016). Racial, gender wage gaps persist in U.S. despite some progress. *Pew Research Center.* Retrieved from http://www.pewresearch.org/fact-tank/2016/07/01/racial-gender-wage-gaps-persist-in-u-s-despite-some-progress/

Patterson, S. (1953). *Colour and culture in South Africa.* New York, NY: Routledge.

Pauls, E. P. (2008). The difference between a tribe and a band: Indigenous people. In *Encyclopedia Britannica.* Retrieved from https://www.britannica.com/topic/Difference-Between-a-Tribe-and-a-Band-1673365

Pelka, F. (2012). *What we have done: An oral history of the disability rights movement.* Amherst, MA: University of Massachusetts Press.

Perrinet, L. U., & Bednar, J. A. (2015). Edge co-occurrences can account for rapid categorization of natural versus animal images. *Scientific Reports, 5*(11400). doi:10.1038/srep11400.

Pharr, S. (1993). Racist politics and homophobia. *Transformation, 8*(4), 1–7, 10.

Pharr, S. (1997). *Homophobia: A weapon of sexism* (2nd ed., expanded ed.). Berkeley, CA: Chardon Press.

Pinderhughes, E. (1989). *Understanding race, ethnicity, and power: The key to efficacy in clinical practice.* New York, NY: Free Press.

Pipher, M. (1994). *Reviving Ophelia: Saving the selves of adolescent girls.* New York, NY: Ballantine Books.

Plessy v. Ferguson 163 U.S. 537 (1896).

Pollack, W., & Shuster, T. (2000). *Real boys' voices.* New York, NY: Penguin.

Population. (2017). *Fanack Chronicle of the Middle East & North Africa.* Retrieved from https://chronicle.fanack.com/united-arab-emirates/population/

Posel, D. (2001). Race as common sense: Racial classification in twentieth-century South Africa. *African Studies Review, 44*(2), 87–113.

Poston, W. S. C. (1990). The biracial identity development model: A needed addition. *Journal of Counseling and Development, 69*, 152–155.

Project Concern International. (n.d.). *Women's empowerment & poverty.* Retrieved from https://www.pciglobal.org/womens-empowerment-poverty/

Project Implicit. (n.d.). Retrieved from https://implicit.harvard.edu/implicit/takeatest.html

Rao, J. (2010). The caste system: Effects on poverty in India, Nepal and Sri Lanka. *Global Majority E-Journal, 1*(2), 97–106. Retrieved from https://www.american.edu/cas/economics/ejournal/upload/Global_Majority_e_Journal_1-2_Rao.pdf.

Reagon, B. J. (2000). Section 3. Coalition. In J. F. Perea, R. Delgado, A. Harris, & S. M. Wildman (Eds.), *Race and races: Cases and resources for a diverse America* (pp. 1104–1109). St. Paul, MN: West Group.

Reeves, R.V. (2017). *Dream hoarders: How the American upper middle class is leaving everyone else in the dust, why that is a problem, and what to do about it.* Washington, DC: Brookings Institute Press.

Rehabilitation Act of 1973, 29 U.S.C. § 701 et seq. (2006).

Reimer, L. E. (2014). Conflict transformation: Canadian democracy and aboriginal relations, *Global Journal of Peace Research and Praxis, 1*(1), 32–45.

Reimer, L. E., Schmitz, C. L., Janke, E. M., Askerov, A., Strahl, B. T., & Matyók, T. (2015). *Transformative change: An introduction to peace and conflict studies.* Lanham, MD: Lexington Books.

Renn, K. A. (2012). Creating and re-creating race: The emergence of racial identity as a critical element in psychological, sociological, and ecological perspectives on human development. In C. L. Wijeyesinghe & B. W. Jackson III (Eds.), *New perspectives on racial identity development: Integrating emerging frameworks* (2nd ed., pp. 11–32*).* New York, NY: New York University Press.

Rochquemore, K., & Laszloffy, T. (2005). *Raising biracial children* (1st ed.). Lanham, MD: AltaMira Press.

Root, M. P. P. (2003). Five mixed-race identities: From relic to revolution. In L. I. Winters & H. L. DeBose (Eds.), *New faces in a changing America* (pp. 3–20). Thousand Oaks, CA: Sage.

Rosaldo, R. (1993). *Culture and truth: The remaking of social analysis.* Boston, MA: Beacon.

Roser, M., & Ortiz-Ospina, E. (2017). *Global extreme poverty.* Retrieved from https://ourworldindata.org/extreme-poverty/

Rothman, J. C. (2003). *Social work practice: Across disability.* Boston, MA: Allyn & Bacon.

Rothstein, R. (2017). *The color of law: A forgotten history of how our government segregated America.* New York, NY: Liveright.

Russo, F. (2016). Is there something unique about the transgender brain? *Scientific American Mind*. Retrieved from http://www.scientificamerican.com/article/is-there-something-unique-about-the-transgender-brain/

Saikia, N., Bora, J. K., Jasilionis, D., & Shkolnikov, M. M. (2016). Disability Divides in India: Evidence from the 2011 Census. *PLoS ONE, 11*(8), e0159809. Retrieved from https://doi.org/10.1371/journal.pone.0159809

Saleebey, D. (1994). Culture, theory, and narrative: The intersection of meaning in practice. *Social Work, 39*(4), 351–359.

Saleebey, D. (2002). Introduction: Power in the people. In D. Saleebey (Ed.), *The strengths perspective in social work practice* (pp. 1–22). Boston, MA: Allyn & Bacon.

Samuels, G. M. (2009). Being raised by white people: Navigating racial difference among adopted multiracial adults. *Journal of Marriage and Family, 71*(1), 80–94.

Samuels, G. M. (2014). Multiethnic and multiracialism. In *Encyclopedia of social work*. Retrieved from http://socialwork.oxfordre.com/view/10.1093/acrefore/9780199975839.001.0001/acrefore-9780199975839-e-991

Sankaran, S., Sekerdej, M., & Von Hecker, U. (2017). The role of Indian caste identity and caste inconsistent norms on status representation. *Frontiers in Psychology: Personality and Social Psychology, 8*(487), doi:10.3389/fpsyg.2017.00487.

Schirch, L., & Campt, D. (2007). *The little book of dialogue for difficult subjects*. Intercourse, PA: Good Books.

Schmitz, C. L., Matyók, T., James, C. D., & Sloan, L. M. (2013). Environmental sustainability: Educating social workers for interdisciplinary practice. In M. Gray, J. Coates, & T. Hetherington, *Environmental social work* (pp. 260–279). New York, NY: Routledge.

Schmitz, C. L., Stakeman, C., & Sisneros, J. (2001). Educating professionals for practice in a multicultural society: Understanding oppression and valuing diversity. *Families in Society, 82*(6), 612–622.

Schmitz, C. L., Vazquez Jacobus, M., Stakeman, C., Valenzuela, G., & Sprankel, J. (2003). Immigrant and refugee communities: Resiliency, trauma, and social work practice. *Social Thought, 22*(2/3), 135–158.

Schofield, T. P., Deckman, T., Garris, C. P., DeWall, C. N., & Denson, T. F. (2015). Brief report: Evidence of ingroup bias on the shooter task in a Saudi sample. *SAGE Open, 5*(1), 1–6.

Schwartz, S. J., Zamboanga, B. L., Meca, A., & Ritchie, R. A. (2012). Identity around the world: An overview. *New Directions for Child and Adolescent Development, 212*(138), 1–18. doi:10.1002/cad.20019.

Schwartz, S. J., Zamboanga, B. L., Weisskirch, R. S., & Rodriguez, L. (2009). The relationships of personal and ethnic identity exploration to indices of adaptive and maladaptive psychosocial functioning. *International Journal of Behavioral Development, 33*, 131–144.

Schweik, S. M. (2009). *The ugly laws: Disability in public*. New York, NY: New York University Press.

Scutti, S. (2014). Becoming transsexual: Getting the facts on sex reassignment surgery. *The Grapevine*. Retrieved from http://www.medicaldaily.com/becoming-transsexual-getting-facts-sex-reassignment-surgery-309584

Seale, A., Bains, A., & Avrett, S. (2010). Partnership, sex, and marginalization: Moving the global fund sexual orientation and gender identities agenda. *Health and Human Rights Journal, 12*(1), 123.

Seller, R. M., Smith, R. A., Shelton, J. N., Rowley, S. A. J., & Chavous, T. M. (1998). Multidimensional model of racial identity: A reconceptualization of African American racial identity. *Personality and Social Psychology Review, 2*(1), 18–39.

Senehi, J. (2002). Constructive storytelling: A peace process. *Peace and Conflict Studies, 9*(2), 41–63.

Senehi, J., Flaherty, M., Kirupakaran, C. S., Kornelsen, L., Matenge, M., & Skarlato, O. (2009). Dreams of our grandmothers: Discovering the call for social justice through storytelling. *Storytelling, Self, Society: An Interdisciplinary Journal of Storytelling Studies, 5*(2), 90–106.

Seuffert, N. (2009). Reflections on transgender immigration. *Griffith Law Review, 18*(2), 428–452.

Sharp, Gene. (1973). *198 methods of non-violent action.* Retrieved from http://www. aforcemorepowerful.org/resources/nonviolent/methods.php

Singh, H. (2008, April 21). The real world of caste in India. *The Journal of Peasant Studies, 35*(1), 119–132.

Skarpenes, O., & Sakslind, R. (2010). Education and egalitarianism: The culture of the Norwegian middle class. *The Sociological Review, 58*(2), 219–243.

Smedley, A. (2007). *Race in North America: Origin and evolution of a worldview* (3rd ed.). Boulder, CO: Westview Press.

Smith, B. (1993). Homophobia: Why bring it up? *Interracial Books for Children Bulletin, 14*(3/4), 7–8.

Smith, B., & Smith, B. (1983). Across the kitchen table. In C. Moraga & G. Anzaldua (Eds.), *This bridge called my back: Writings by radical women of color* (2nd ed., pp. 113–127). New York, NY: Kitchen Table, Women of Color Press.

Smith, T. B., & Silva, L. (2011). Ethnic identity and personal well-being of people of color: A meta-analysis. *Journal of Counseling Psychology, 58,* 42–60.

Snow, K. (2016). *A hierarchy of disability.* Retrieved from https://www.disabilityisnatural. com/disability-hierarchy-1.html

Snyder, T. (2017). *On tyranny: Twenty lessons from the twentieth century.* New York, NY: The Duggan Books.

Somech, A., & Drach-Zahavy, A. (2016). Gender role ideology. *The Wiley Blackwell encyclopedia of gender and sexuality studies.* Retrieved from http://onlinelibrary.wiley. com/doi/10.1002/9781118663219.wbegss205/abstract

Soylu, A., & Buchanon, T. A. (2013). Ethnic and racial discrimination against immigrants. *Journal of Business and Economics, 4*(9), 8548–8581.

Spurlin, W. J. (2010). Resisting heteronormativity/resisting recolonisation: Affective bonds between indigenous women in southern Africa and the difference(s) of postcolonial feminist history. *Feminist Review, 95*(95), 10–26.

Staats, C., Capatosto, K., Wright, R. A., & Jackson, V. W. (2016). *Implicit racial bias and school discipline disparities: Exploring the connection.* Retrieved from http:// kirwaninstitute.osu.edu/wp-content/uploads/2016/07/implicit-bias-2016.pdf

Stone, D., Patton, B., & Heen, S. (2010). *Difficult conversations: How to discuss what matters most.* New York, NY: Penguin Books.

Stone, O., & Kusnick, P. (2013). *The untold history of the United States.* New York, NY: Gallery Books.

Strides in Development. (2010). *Wangari Maathai & the green belt movement.* [Video file]. Retrieved from https://m.youtube.com/watch?v=BQU7JOxkGvo

Stroman, D. F. (2003). *The disability rights movement: From deinstitutionalization to self-determination.* New York, NY: University Press of America.

Sue, D., & Sue, D. W. (1993). Ethnic identity: Cultural factors in the psychological devel-opment of Asians in America. In D. R. Atkinson, G. Morten, & D. W. Sue (Eds.), *Counseling American minorities: A cross-cultural perspective* (4th ed., pp. 199–210). Madison, WI: Brown & Benchmark.

Sue, D. W. (2003). *Overcoming our racism: The journey to liberation*. San Francisco, CA: Jossey-Bass.

Sue, D. W., & Sue, D. (2016). *Counseling the culturally diverse: Theory and practice* (7rd ed.). Hoboken, NJ: John Wiley and Sons.

Syed, M., Walker, L. H. M., Lee, R. M., Umaña-Taylor, A. J., Zamboanga, B. L., Schwartz, S. J., Armenta, B. E., & Huynh, Q. (2013). A two-factor model of ethnic iden-tity exploration: Implications for identity coherence and well-being. *Cultural Diversity and Ethnic Minority Psychology, 19*(2), 143–154.

Szegedy-Maszak, M. (2001). The power of gender. *U.S. News & World Report, 130*(22), 52.

Takaki, R. (2008). *A different mirror: A history of multicultural America* (Rev. ed.). Boston, MA: Little, Brown and Company.

Tarek, M. (2005). The baby with Down syndrome. *Ain Shams Journal of Obstetrics and Gynecology, 2,* 362–365.

Tatum, B. D. (1994). Teaching white students about racism: The search for white allies and the restoration of hope. *Teachers College Record, 94*(4), 462–476.

Tatum, B. D. (2003). *Why are all the black kids sitting together in the cafeteria?* New York, NY: Basic Books.

Taylor, Y. (2009). Complexities and complications: Intersections of class and sexuality. *Journal of Lesbian Studies, 13*(2), 189–203.

Testa, R.J., Jimenez, C.L., & Rankin, S. (2013). Risk and resilience during transgender identity development: The effects of awareness and engagement with other transgender people on affect. *Journal of Gay and Lesbian Mental Health, 18*(1), 31–36.

Thompson, D. (2011). *Ugly laws: The history of disability regulation in North America.* Retrieved http://www.ambest.com/directories/bestconnect/DeeGeeArticle.pdf

Thomson, R. G. (Ed.). (1997). *Extraordinary bodies: Figuring physical disability in American culture and literature.* New York, NY: Columbia University Press.

Transgender Europe. (n.d.).*Violence & hate speech.* Retrieved from http://tgeu.org/issues/violence-hate-speech

Trent, J. (2016). *Inventing the feeble mind: A history of intellectual disability in the United States* (2nd ed.). New York, NY: Oxford University Press.

Tribe. (2017). In *Oxford Dictionary.* Retrieved from https://en.oxforddictionaries.com/definition/tribe

Tucker, J., & Lowell, C. (2016, September). *National snapshot: Poverty among women & families, 2015.* Retrieved from https://nwlc.org/wp-content/uploads/2016/09/Poverty-Snapshot-Factsheet-2016.pdf

Tully, C. T. (2000). *Lesbians, gays, and the empowerment perspective.* New York, NY: Columbia University Press.

Tumin, M. M. (1953). Some principles of stratification: A critical analysis. *American Sociological Review, 18*(4), 387–394.

Tumin, M. M. (1984). *Social stratification: The forms and functions of inequality* (2nd ed.). Upper Saddle River, NJ: Prentice-Hall.

United Nations. (2004). *Nothing about us, without us.* Retrieved from http://www.un.org/esa/socdev/enable/iddp2004.htm

United Nations. (2006). Convention on the Rights of Persons with Disabilities (CRPD), *Division for Social Policy and Development.* Retrieved from https://www.un.org/

development/desa/disabilities/convention-on-the-rights-of-persons-with-disabilities/preamble.html

United Nations. (2013). *The millennium development goals report, 2013* [PDF file]. Retrieved from www.un.org/millenniumgoals/pdf/report-2013/mdg-report-2013-english.pdf

United Nations. (2015). *The world's women 2015: Trends and statistics.* Retrieved from https://unstats.un.org/unsd/gender/worldswomen.html

United Nations Department of Economic and Social Affairs. (2016). *International Migration Report 2015: Highlights.* Retrieved from http://www.un.org/en/development/desa/population/migration/publications/migrationreport/docs/MigrationReport2015_Highlights.pdf

United Nations Economic and Security Council (UNESCO). (1950). *Brief communications: UNESCO statement by experts on problems of race.* Retrieved from http.//unesdoc.unesco.org/images/0012/001269/126969eb.pdf

United Nations. (2017). *Free and equal: Transgender* [PDF file]. Retrieved from https://www.unfe.org/wp-content/uploads/2017/05/UNFE-Transgender.pdf

United Nations High Commission on Refugees (UNHCR). (2017). *Figures at a glance.* Retrieved from http://www.unhcr.org/figures-at-a-glance.html

United Nations. (2017). *Speak up, stop discrimination: Combatting discrimination against migrants.* Retrieved from http://www.ohchr.org/EN/Issues/Discrimination/Pages/discrimination_migrants.aspx

United Nations. (n.d.). *Facts and figures: Ending violence against women.* Retrieved from http://www.unwomen.org/en/what-we-do/ending-violence-against-women/facts-and-figures

United States v. Schwartz, 82 F Supp.933 (D.C. 1949).

US Commission on Civil Rights. (2004, September). *Broken promises: Evaluating the Native American health care system.* Retrieved from http://www.usccr.gov/pubs/nahealth/nabroken.pdf

Van Soest, D. (2003). Advancing social and economic justice. In D. Lum (Ed.), *Culturally competent practice: A framework for understanding diverse groups and justice issues* (2nd ed., pp. 345–376). Pacific Grove, CA: Brooks/Cole.

Van Wormer, K. (1994). A society without poverty: The Norwegian experience. *Social Work, 39,* 324–327.

Vertovec, S., & Wessendorf, S. (Eds.). (2010). *The multiculturalism backlash. European discourses, policies and practices.* New York, NY: Routledge.

Waller, M., & Yellow Bird, M. (2002). Strengths of First Nations peoples. In D. Saleebey (Ed.), *The strengths perspective in social work practice* (pp. 48–62). Boston, MA: Allyn & Bacon.

Walters, K. L., Longres, J. F., Han, C.-S., & Icard, L. D. (2003). Cultural competence with gay and lesbian persons of color. In D. Lum (Ed.), *Culturally competent practice: A framework for understanding diverse groups and justice issues* (2nd ed., pp. 310–342). Pacific Grove, CA: Brooks/Cole.

Washington, P. A., & Harris, B. J. (2001). Women of color standpoints: Introduction. *NWSA Journal, 13*(2), 80–83.

WaterAid.(2016).Overflowingcities:Thestateoftheworld'stoilet2016.Retrievedfromhttp://wateraidindia.in/publication/overflowing-cities-state-worlds-toilet-2016/

Weaver, H. N. (2017). Disability through a Native American lens: Examining influences of culture and colonization. In H. N. Weaver & F. K. Yuen (Eds.), *All my relations: Understanding the experiences of Native Americans with disabilities* (pp. 148–162). New York, NY: Routledge.

Weinman, S. (1984). *The politics of human services: Radical alternatives to the welfare state.* Boston, MA: South End Press.

White, F. E. (2001). *Dark continent of our bodies: Black feminism and the politics of respectability.* Philadelphia, PA: Temple University Press.

Wijeyesinghe, C. L. (2001). Racial identity in multiracial people: An alternative paradigm. In C. L. Wijeyesinghe & B. W. Jackson III (Eds.), *New perspectives on racial identity development: A theoretical and practical anthology* (pp. 129–152). New York, NY: New York University Press.

Wijeyesinghe, C. L. (2012). The intersectional model of multiracial identity? Integrating multiracial identity theories and intersectional perspectives on social identity. In C. L. Wijeyesinghe & B. W. Jackson III (Eds.). *New perspectives on racial identity development: Integrating emerging frameworks* (2nd ed., pp. 81–107). New York, NY: New York University Press.

Wijeyesinghe, C. L., & Jackson, B. W. III (Eds.) (2012). *New perspectives on racial identity development: Integrating emerging frameworks* (2nd ed.). New York, NY: New York University Press.

Wildman, S. M., & Davis, A. D. (2002). Making systems of privilege visible. In P. Rothenberg (Ed.), *White privilege essential readings on the other side of racism* (pp. 85–95). New York, NY: Worth.

Williams, T. (2012). *Understanding internalized oppression: A theoretical conceptualization of internalized subordination* (Doctoral dissertation). University of Massachusetts, Amherst, Massachusetts. Retrieved from http://scholarworks.umass.edu/cgi/viewcontent.cgi?article=1628&context=open_access_dissertations

Wilson, A. (2013). Feminism in the space of the world social forum. *Journal of International Women's Studies, 8*(3), 10–27.

Wimmer, A. (2008, August 19). Elementary strategies of ethnic boundary making. *Ethnic and Racial Studies, 31*(6), 1025–1055.

World Bank. (2016). *World development indicators 2016.* Washington, DC: World Bank Group. Retrieved from http://documents.worldbank.org/curated/en/805371467990952829/World-development-indicators-2016

World Commission on Environment and Development. (1987). *Our common future.* New York, NY: Oxford University Press.

World Health Organization (WHO). (2011). *Summary: World report on disabilities.* Retrieved from http://www.who.int/disabilities/world_report/2011/en/

Wren, B. (2000). Early physical intervention for young people with atypical gender identity development. *Clinical Child Psychology and Psychiatry, 5*(2), 220–231.

Xin, M. (2012). Political capital and wealth accumulation. In R. Garnaut & L. Song (Eds.), *China: New engine of world growth* (pp. 316–329). ANU Press. Retrieved from http://www.jstor.org/stable/j.ctt24h9qh

Young, I. (2004). Five faces of oppression. In L. Heldke & P. O'Connor (Eds.), *Oppression, privilege, & resistance* (pp. 37–63). Boston, MA: McGraw Hill.

Young, I. M. (1990). *Justice and the politics of difference.* Princeton, NJ: Princeton University Press.

Young, I. M. (2000). Difference as a resource for democratic communication. In A. Anton, M. Fisk, & N. Holstrum. (Eds.), *Not for sale* (pp. 109–131), Boulder, CO: Westview Press.

Young, I. M. (2011). *Justice and the politics of difference.* Princeton, NJ: Princeton University Press.

Yudell, M. (2014). *Race unmasked: Biology and race in the twentieth century.* New York, NY: Columbia University Press.

Zehr, H. (2002). *The little book of restorative justice*. Intercourse, PA: Good Books.

Zerjal, T., Spencer Wells, R., Yuldasheva, N., Ruzibakiev, R., & Tyler-Smith, C. (2002). A genetic landscape reshaped by recent events: Y-chromosomal insights into Central Asia. *American Journal of Human Genetics, 7*, 466–482.

Zinn, H. (2015). *A people's history of the United States: 1492–present* (3rd ed.). New York, NY: Routledge. (Original work published in 1980)

INDEX

Page numbers followed by *f, t,* and *b* refer to figures, tables, and boxes, respectively.

Made in the USA
Columbia, SC
15 January 2021